D

# WHY JOIN A
# TRADE UNION?

ALSO BY JO PHILLIPS AND DAVID SEYMOUR

*Why Vote? A guide to those who can't be bothered*

# WHY JOIN A TRADE UNION?

Jo Phillips and
David Seymour

**biteback** ⌄⌄
⌃⌃

First published in Great Britain in 2010 by
Biteback Publishing Ltd
Heal House
375 Kennington Lane
London
SE11 5QY

ISBN 978-1-84954-068-1

10 9 8 7 6 5 4 3 2 1

A CIP catalogue record for this book is available from the British Library.

Set in Charter and Rockwell by SoapBox
Printed and bound in Great Britain by CPI Cox & Wyman, Reading, RG1 8EX

# Contents

# Preface

In case you haven't noticed, we stand at a crossroads. There is a new kind of government in power and with it such massive changes to the way we have grown used to living that we may wake up in a few years and find we hardly recognise our society.

Technology is changing, the world is changing, and the pressures on young people, the elderly and just about everyone in between are being ratcheted up several notches.

Work is changing, too. What we do, when we do it, how we do it – and if it is there for us to do.

Rather lost in this blizzard of change are the trade unions. A generation ago they were central to life in this country. Today they seem an irrelevancy at best and, at worst, a reactionary irritant.

Yet unions not only have a noble past (interspersed with some decidedly ignoble episodes); they might, just might, have a crucial part to play as we weave through the challenges of the next decades.

Are they dinosaurs lumbering inexorably to extinction? Or a superman poised to swoop and save the planet? Members of the jury, you are about to hear the evidence.

# A marriage of inconvenience

Unless you have inherited a fortune or won the jackpot on the Lottery or you are a hermit living on grass and rain water, the chances are you will spend roughly a quarter of your life at work because that is the only way to earn money. At least, the only legal way.

This is how work works. You sell your labour and skills. In return, you get money – the middle classes call it income, the working classes wages.

Sounds like a pretty straightforward idea, doesn't it? Yet it has tied up political theorists, social campaigners and philosophers for centuries. At the heart of their agonising is the relationship between the employee and the employer. Like marriage, it can be fraught with tension and often is.

It doesn't matter whether you are a city banker or a part-time cleaner, usually you work because you need the money to live (some people work because they love working – this book is not for them; they should seek the help of a good psychiatrist). You are therefore dependent on your employer, who can bully, threaten or exploit you (or all three). Beastly bosses have been around forever and sadly will be until Judgment Day. And considering some of the underhand, devious tricks they get away with, they will probably even survive that.

One thing stands between workers being trampled over

as they were for centuries and a working life that provides at least a modicum of dignity, decent conditions and reasonable pay. And that is the trade unions. They are the knights on white chargers who give ordinary people the chance of preventing bosses treating their employees badly, even despicably.

At least, that is what the unions and their leaders want you to believe.

It's a big ask. Come on, be honest. Do you believe unions are the great protectors of working people or do you consider them to be the unreasonable, grasping, greedy, smug, backward-looking, bolshie, objectionable bastards who stop your trains running, interfere with your children's education and generally screw up the smooth running of your life while threatening the country with economic disaster?

# The case against

Unions exist to cause mayhem. If airport baggage handlers go on strike, they do it at the peak of the holiday season. Ditto the train drivers over bank holidays. Council workers take industrial action to drag the country back to the dark ages. Even previously respectable professionals have joined in. Teachers, of all people. What do they think they are teaching children when they withdraw their labour?

As for union leaders, they are a sub-human species that should be bracketed with criminals, the dysfunctional and Piers Morgan. If you ask most people to name a union leader they will probably come up with Arthur Scargill or Bob Crow. Scargill, recognisable by his comb-over hairstyle, is the man who took on Maggie Thatcher by leading the bitter year-long miners' strike of 1984–5 and lost.

Bob Crow is a Millwall supporter and looks like one. His dog is called Castro after the Cuban revolutionary leader who is one of Crow's heroes, along with Arthur Scargill. He runs the rail union and is a particular hate figure for Londoners due to his penchant for shutting down the Tube system (an unnecessary task, as it shuts down of its own volition for much of the time). This is known to newspaper headline writers as 'commuter chaos' or 'travel misery for millions'. A cynic might wonder if the ballot papers have already been printed for a walkout just before the 2012 Olympics.

So, two die-hard left wingers who match every prejudice about union leaders including the language they use: they talk about comrades, walkouts, solidarity, the overthrow of the ruling classes and fighting the cuts. For them, the revolution is always just around the corner. Unlike the train driven by one of Bob Crow's members during a period of industrial unrest.

# The case for

There is a silly game beloved of management consultants in which a group of people sit in a circle and have to find out about the person next to them. If you played a variation of that when you were in the street or on the bus or in the supermarket, one of the surprising things you would discover about those seemingly normal human beings around you is how many belong to a union. More than six million at the latest count. It used to be almost double that but even so it is, you must agree, a pretty sizeable section of the British population.

What's more, they look ordinary, don't have two heads or webbed feet and almost certainly share your frustration and annoyance when trade union action disrupts daily life.

Odd as it may seem when public opinion often reflects the bile poured out from the press, unions weren't invented to cause irritation and disruption to other people. On the contrary. The reason for their existence is to do things for other people. They are based on the concept that campaigning together for something, or against it, will have more clout than one lone voice. Particularly when dealing with mercenary and unscrupulous employers. If the only power you have is your labour then you'd be daft not to use that power by withdrawing your labour when you are pushed to the edge.

Unions have fought for better working conditions in factories, farms, hospitals, call centres, schools, building sites and government offices. They've campaigned for the right of people to sick pay and maternity leave, paid holidays and safety at work. They have a long and proud history of providing education for people who otherwise would have had no access to it.

They've fought for equal rights and reasonable working hours and have stood up to bullies. Having battled to extend the franchise, unions created a party that working people could vote for (the Labour Party, in case that description of Labour passes you by).

OK, they have made governments quake and prime ministers fume and brought the country almost to its knees on rare occasions. But without them, ordinary people would be a lot worse off.

Members of the jury, that is the case for the defence.

## Can't see the join?

Everyone in the UK has the right to join a trade union. You may have an employer who tries to stop you but ultimately it's nothing to do with him whether you do or indeed which union you join. Obviously it makes sense to belong to one that's relevant to your particular trade or profession. If you work in banking, for instance, it's not a terribly good idea to try to join NACODS, the National Association of Colliery Overmen, Deputies and Shotfirers. (Try BIFU – the Banking, Insurance and Finance Union – instead, which to add to the confusion has been merged into Unite.)

Those six million UK union members work in every trade and profession from nurses and engineers to footballers and sheep shearers. That's about one in six of everyone who's working. Although it's only half what it was in the 1970s part of that is due to working life, just like everything else, changing since then, as anyone who's watched *Ashes to Ashes* can tell you. And if you think that's a TV programme about cricket Tests between England and Australia, you clearly haven't watched it.

One reason union membership has fallen so steeply is that, in those days, you often couldn't get a job unless you joined one. That was the closed shop – closed to non-union members. This did a lot to boost union membership – if you didn't join, you didn't work. It also made the unions extremely powerful, particularly in manufacturing and heavy industry but in all sorts of other areas, including the media and the arts.

The Tories, employers and right-wingers everywhere saw this as a great plot. They argued that the unions were bullies, forcing people to join so they could work and then using membership fees to support the Labour Party, which

The historic meeting of the Midlands Area Brick Makers' Union when they voted overwhelmingly to change their slogan to 'United We Sit'.

they did all they could to dominate and dictate to. It was a take-over of the government and the country by the back door.

There was another side to this, which you never read about in the papers. If you were one of the millions who felt disenfranchised by the control the establishment had over every part of the country, it didn't seem too bad that people who represented you were in there fighting on your behalf, however dirtily.

Of course, it wasn't like this in reality. The unions never achieved the control the hysterics claimed they had and, anyway, there was rarely any indication that they had any positive influence on the Labour Party, let alone the

7

government, though at times they had a major negative influence which kept Labour firmly out of power.

Eventually, in the early 1990s and after a series of laws that removed many of the powers of the unions, the closed shop was made illegal. This was done by Margaret Thatcher.

You may now hiss.

# Back to the future

There was a time when people could rely on having a job for life. That luxury has gone forever. In future it is unlikely that all but a tiny minority of us will stay in the same job from the moment we leave education to the day we retire.

Throughout that major part of our lives, the pattern will be of periods of temporary or contract work, spells of unemployment, changes of career, dipping into part-time work, having more than one job at a time and continuing to work well into our sixties. The frightening pace of change requires a modern, flexible labour force. The skills that are needed will be in high demand and will be well rewarded. But while the old skills that were the backbone of industry in the nineteenth century, and much of the twentieth, faded out slowly, the skills of today may disappear almost overnight and, with them, the workers who performed them.

A recent survey among young people showed that six of

the ten jobs they most wished to do didn't exist a decade ago. Patterns of work have changed radically, too.

The TUC, the Trades Union Congress, the umbrella organisation for unions, used to be portrayed as a cart-horse; it was considered to be too slow to move with the times. And that was half a century ago. So the challenges which face the unions nowadays, when speed of travel isn't measured in horsepower but some sort of electronic giga-thingy, is overwhelming.

That doesn't necessarily mean they are as pointless as a ton of coal in the desert. On the contrary, there is an argument that the new freedoms which have brought fresh anxieties about job security and much else can only be satisfactorily dealt with by working together, just as the need was for the downtrodden of previous centuries to get the help of the unions.

The comparative economic stability of our lifetime means that most of us take for granted the idea that we can go to work, do our job and get paid reasonably for it. We expect our workplace, whether that's a construction site or a call centre, to be safe and free from hazards. We don't go to work to be bullied, threatened or sexually har-assed. We expect to be treated fairly and, if we're not, to be able to complain without fear of intimidation. Why? Because we are protected by employment law, much of which has come about as a result of trade union pressure.

So let us accept that they have done the hard bit. Is this now the time to bid them farewell and pack them off to retirement in a nice little home by the seaside where they can natter all day long about the Good Old Days?

In other words: do we still need them, why should we feed them, now they're a hundred and sixty four?

## Smokestacks to motherboards

When people talk about the death of manufacturing, it's as though a sepia tint falls over Britain and we are transported to a Hovis ad where hundreds of cheery factory workers head off on their bikes to the allotments after a hard day *making something*.

In the late 1970s, manufacturing provided jobs for almost a third of the UK's workforce and accounted for 30 per cent of our gross domestic product. Today it's less than half that. Quite simply, ships, planes, cars, tractors, machinery, furniture, pottery, clothing and steel can be produced somewhere else in the world for less money. A lot less.

The former cotton mills, potteries and dockyards are more likely to be the hub of 'creative quarters' which have proved so valuable to the regeneration of towns and cities. Tin mines and goods sheds have become restaurants while buildings that once housed great engines and hundreds of workers are now museums where you can experience the discomfort of hard physical labour for a few minutes before going to the souvenir shop.

This different sort of industrial revolution, coupled with globalisation, has changed the way we work, buy and sell. Such huge changes left their mark on communities where once virtually everyone worked for one employer, whether that was a shipyard, coal mine or food-processing plant.

Even the most powerful and organised unions lost the battle to preserve jobs in traditional manufacturing as the global tide of cheap labour and 24/7 communications swept away old jobs, leaving millions of people high and dry. There are many who would argue that the trade unions let their members down by failing to recognise that change was inevitable and, with that change, different working conditions, different skills and different challenges would be inevitable. The largely manual labour force from old-style manufacturing was ill equipped to adapt and was simply elbowed out of the way by highly skilled people who could do the same job in another country – or here – for lower wages without the likelihood of disruptive industrial action.

We needed and received higher wages because we wanted to enjoy the many pleasures of life which opened up to us: foreign holidays, cars, new furniture for our own homes, eating out regularly, lots of fashionable clothes. So more and more employers decided British workers could enjoy what they wanted but the work they had been doing would go to people who were content to grub along on a far more basic lifestyle (it won't last, they'll want the good life too; but by then it may be too late for us).

British manufacturing adapted by playing to its strengths of design, technology, creativity, innovation and service. But that rarely involved actually manufacturing anything in the traditional sense of the word. The future is being built on those new strengths and skills while factories and heavy industries are consigned to history along with the people who worked in them and the unions who represented them.

Working in a call centre may be unspeakably dull and the duty supervisor a nightmare but the conditions in it cannot be compared to factory work of thirty years ago, let alone Victorian times, when people risked injury, long-term health problems and death every day.

As industry has diversified so too have the demands and concerns of workers. Grievances against employers are now as likely to be about bullying and stress as unreasonable hours or dangerous machinery. Health and safety laws, the minimum wage, equality legislation and European rules have, to a large extent, resolved many of the issues that topped the unions' campaign agenda for years.

Which brings us back to the question: is it time to pension off the unions?

# Left far behind

Just as there are some people who yearn for the good old days of early closing, 'God Save the Queen' played every night as the TV shuts down and roast beef on Sundays, there are those who still dream of class war and the overthrow of capitalism. They are few in number but may be found in student common rooms, the left-wing fringe parties and even in the Labour Party, though rarely in the House of Commons. And some may be tracked down in the trade unions.

That isn't the impression you will get from most of the media. If you believe what you read and hear, the unions still incite totally unreconstructed revolutionaries who sleep with Marx under the pillow while dreaming of storming the bastions of the establishment, such as the House of Lords, Buckingham Palace and the studios of CBeebies, from where capitalist propaganda is pumped into the tender young brains of future citizens.

The vast majority of trade unionists were never like that and even fewer are today. Trade unionists are ordinary people who realise that life has changed, work has changed and the UK has changed, as indeed has the whole world. We may know more about Africa or America than a small village at the other end of our own country. We buy goods ranging from cars and fridges to shoes and phones that are made in China, India, Vietnam or Poland. We purchase food that is flown in from all over the world so we can eat strawberries in December – in fact, whatever food we feel like whatever season it is.

You have got to be pretty blinkered not to accept that when life changes so much, work does too. And it has. Most of us who work do so in relatively safe, clean environments. We are entitled to paid holidays and sick pay, parental leave and a minimum wage. We can't be discriminated against because of the colour of our skin, our sex, age, faith or disability.

On just about every count we are hugely better off than the majority of the people who now produce the things we buy (in fact, it is impossible to think of a single count we're not better off than – with the exception of Count Dracula, should you like drinking blood). The clothes we buy so cheaply in the High Street may be made by children in Asian sweatshops. Those delicious green beans might be grown by Kenyan farmers earning a pittance. Countless millions receive subsistence-level wages or below, work in appalling conditions with virtually no time off and can be fired at whim.

The reason we are so much better off isn't because British employers are capitalistic saints, enlightened bosses who skip among their workers distributing fat pay packets and begging them to work shorter hours and take longer holidays. It is because of the men and women who campaigned, marched, fought, suffered and even died to get better working conditions. So don't be smug about what we have got. And don't be dismissive of how we got it.

Nor should you think for a moment that we can now be complacent. Just because working life is so much better here than in many parts of the world doesn't mean we can relax. Campaigners who talk about wanting to put themselves out of business are striving to find a cure for cancer or end global poverty. When they have achieved their goal, they can pat themselves on the back, pick up their Nobel Prize and retire to a cottage in Dorset.

But it's impossible to foresee a time when trade unions could say: 'That's it, no one will ever be bullied, unfairly sacked or forced to work in dirty and dangerous conditions for rubbish wages again. We've achieved everything so we can pack up and go off to lie on a Cuban beach.' (Geographical note: Cuba is where left-wing union leaders are said to spend their holidays.)

Despite the improvements for British workers over the past century, we work the longest hours in Europe, enjoy far less job security in the current global economic climate and have growing worries about when we can retire and what we'll live on when we do. The pressure to put more hours in, to be on call by phone or email and to learn new skills, meet targets, increase profit margins and cope with changes at work are enormous – in both the public and private sectors.

So here is this confusing conundrum. Unions have achieved a huge amount and there is a lot more still to do. Yet they are despised by large sections of the population who are convinced union leaders are rabid, dangerous socialists who live a life of luxury on salaries many times that of their members and who are determined to end our way of life.

They think (if they do actually think) that unions are old fashioned and dull, with only one purpose to their existence, which is to go on strike as often and inconveniently as possible.

It is said that this is partly due to memories of the strikes of the 1970s. Yet more than half the population can't have any memories of them because they weren't born or were too young to discuss the finer points of picketing or the three-day week, when Conservative Prime Minister Edward Heath ordered the electricity to be turned off to illustrate what life was like when it was dark. The result was that he lost the 'Who Governs Britain?' election that he called in February 1974 (the voters' answer being: 'Not you, mate') and the birth-rate soared nine months later – well, what else can you do when there are no lights and no TV? (Question: if you were conceived during the three-day week, would you instinctively vote Labour or Conservative?)

Other reasons given for unions being hated is that they are considered to prefer confrontation to discussion, rather like that yob in the bar who wants to fight every Friday night. Or that employers are always reasonable and in the right, while it is Neanderthal employees who are out to cause trouble and would go around smashing up looms as the Luddites did a couple of hundred years ago if they could only find some.

# Fear and loathing

Here is a fact. Many more of us have been inconvenienced by industrial action than taken part in it. There are remarkably few strikes nowadays and widespread disruption can be caused by a small number of strikers. For example, if a train driver transported 5,000 passengers a day, a thousand striking drivers would screw up the day for five million people. Of course, that is why industrial action can be so effective. If five million train drivers stopped work for a day and only affected a thousand passengers, it wouldn't bring the employers to their knees, would it? (Legal exemption: if Bob Crow demands as part of his next pay claim that there should be 5,000 drivers on every train to achieve parity with passengers, the publishers of this book accept no liability.)

So much for the loathing widely felt about unions. What about the fear? For that is what some members continue to feel about being seen to be too prominent a part of the union. They worry about being branded troublemakers if they appear too active or supportive of their union. Despite employment laws which protect workers, that concern hasn't gone away. You may suffer victimisation by a thousand snubs and unpleasantries. Even though bosses can't sack you on the spot, they can make your life unbearable, as is all too evident if you sit in for a couple of days on employment tribunals.

There is another fear at work: the reign of terror imposed by unscrupulous employers. Like the ones who run restaurants that use tips to make up staff wages or charge for uniforms. The gang masters who bring in foreign workers and pay them next to nothing. The bullies and sex pests who prey on vulnerable young people and women. The firms that turn a blind eye to health and safety, penalise people for being sick and think nothing of dumping loyal, long-serving staff to cut costs.

It is because of that behaviour and the fear it engenders in employees that unions are so necessary in the workplace. The cartoon image of a big-bellied mill owner bearing down on his cowering, overworked and underpaid employees might be out of date but it has been replaced by profit-mad accountants looking to save every penny even if it means unacceptable workloads or ignoring health and safety or just sacking large numbers of workers.

# A different class

Unions were originally working-class organisations run by working-class people for working-class people. The middle classes thought they had no need of them. They were content to grub along on a pittance doing office or junior managerial work because they considered they were fortunate not to be in one of those gruelling, insecure, badly paid manual jobs.

Over time, though, the middle classes woke up and realised that the working classes, thanks to being organised in unions, were not just closing the gap but had a powerful voice. So they joined in and began to form their own unions. Teachers, council officers, university lecturers, scientists, technical staff, civil servants, journalists – a whole gamut of white-collar workers who lived suburban lives and may well have voted Conservative joined up.

But they maintained a veneer of middle-class gentility. This was the acceptable face of trade unionism. Their representatives negotiated politely, seldom raised their voices and never, but *never*, took industrial action.

Something changed, though, around the middle of the

1970s. Suddenly the white-collar unionists became militant. Horrors! Here were real class traitors. Previously class traitors were the union leaders who sold out their members. Now middle-class employees were accused of betraying *their* class of respectable folk by behaving like. . . well, those ruffian trade unionists.

The media retains a particular opprobrium for strikers such as teachers, council officers or airline cabin crews because, frankly, they simply aren't *expected* to act like that. After all, *they are people like us!* (This makes the assumption that workers in manual industries are some form of sub-species of the human race.)

However, it is inescapably true that since white-collar unionists became more militant, they have improved their pay and conditions in a way they failed to do when they were prepared to be the nice guys of the union movement.

When white-collar unionism was in the embryo stage, it kept itself to itself, perhaps for fear of contamination by contact with the older industrial unions or maybe they didn't want to scare their fledgling members. Then the Manufacturing, Science and Finance union, under the leadership of the entrepreneurial Clive Jenkins, saw the opportunities offered by the burgeoning computer, finance and associated industries.

The Amalgamated Union of Engineering Workers, whose

traditional members certainly had blue collars, except on Sundays, established a separate section for clerical staff in the industries which the union served. It was known as TASS, the Technical, Administrative and Supervisory Section.

Then there was NALGO, the National Association of Local Government Officers, which found a rich seam of recruits in council offices who realised how much the manual employees they were supposed to be managing had gained from union membership. In fact, the biggest growth in union membership now is among public-sector workers.

And so it continued. This growth changed the face of employment and the relationship between bosses and their clerical staff, and it showed workers that just because you wore a white collar didn't mean you had to let yourself be walked all over.

# Life on Mars

If a Martian dropped in and wanted a quick lesson in how the UK has changed over the past half-century, he (it?) could do worse than study what has happened to the unions.

Membership grew steadily after the Second World War and peaked at the end of the 1970s at more than 13 million. Today it is not much over half that figure.

By the time Mrs Thatcher came to power in 1979 the number of strikes had gone down sharply – from 5,000 a year in 1970 to 1,500 – although you wouldn't have thought so to read the papers. By the end of the century it was just a couple of hundred a year.

Now there are thirty times more days lost through injury than there are through industrial action. But you don't hear much about the dangers at work that lead to those injuries, while the papers continue to churn out stories about civilisation-threatening strikes. (The reason for this is that workers are dispensable but nothing must be allowed to interfere with the smooth running of the economy.)

The vast majority of stoppages are in the public sector (94 per cent in 2008). The idea of great British industries being ground to a halt by militant trade unionists is very much a thing of the past (as are great British industries).

But back to our Martian. Let us point out to him the giant Transport and General Workers' Union, which in 1980 had two million members. By the turn of the century, that was down to 700,000 and within a few more years it had merged with Amicus to create Unite.

Unison, the big public-sector union, also saw a decline in membership but it was far less severe, slipping from 1.6 million to 1.3 million over the same period.

Around 30 per cent of employed people are in unions today, compared with more than 50 per cent at the peak.

But we don't do badly in comparison with other countries. The French, for example, who are often held up as the model of militancy, with strikes going on endlessly, have only got 9 per cent of their working population in unions.

# Consumed with anger

There may have been a time when workers were workers and consumers were consumers and never the twain would meet, but it hasn't been like that for some time.

The trade unionist is a user of all those services in which other trade unionists are employed. So his industrial action will affect – and probably annoy – them, and theirs will do the same to him.

The train driver who strikes interferes with the teacher getting to work, while the teacher who strikes stops the train driver's children going to school. The council worker who fails to empty the dustbins of the airline cabin staff has his holiday affected by their strike.

Brotherly (and sisterly) solidarity declares that all trade unionists sympathise with the actions of other trade unionists in their struggles for better pay or conditions, but you're not human if you don't get niggled when your daily routine is disrupted.

Even if you really believe the people who empty your bins are underpaid and exploited, that doesn't mean you merely smile beatifically when they go on strike and your stinking bin isn't emptied for a month during a blazing hot summer.

You may sympathise with how teachers are treated, but when you can't go to work because your kids can't go to school because the teachers have walked out, you're not happy. And neither is your boss (though, thanks to the unions, he can't sack you).

Even though there are fewer trade unionists now than there used to be, there are still a lot. That doesn't mean, though, that one union's industrial action is met with widespread support. Not at all. Strikers are treated as if they are Public Enemy Number One, not just by employers, the CBI and most of the media, but by much of the public.

While for some people this is due to dogmatic opposition to the unions, the left, the Labour Party and so on, it is usually no more than feeling aggrieved that life is being interfered with. *Why can't they be satisfied with what they've got? They should consider themselves lucky to* have *a job*.

In the past few years there has been only one strike that attracted widespread public support and that was when tanker drivers blockaded petrol supplies. They weren't taking action on their own behalf but to bring down the cost of petrol by forcing the government to cut tax on fuel. At least, that's what they said.

For several days, these drivers were unlikely popular heroes, battling on behalf of ordinary people against the harsh taxes imposed by unpopular rulers – rather like Robin Hood did nearly 900 years ago to bring down the twelfth-century equivalent of fuel duty.

Then suddenly the media and public realised the immediate consequences of what the strikers were doing. There was no petrol at the pumps. It became difficult to drive to work or to see the mother-in-law for Sunday lunch, especially when fleets of little old ladies blocked forecourts to fill up with another thimbleful of petrol every time they used some by pootling to the end of their driveway. Within hours, the strike collapsed.

So much for solidarity between strikers and consumers.

# Hate figures 1:
# Maggie, Maggie, Maggie

Where there are unions, there are hate figures. On both sides of the political spectrum.

The great focus for the left remains Margaret Hilda Thatcher. She has remained the nemesis of the trade union movement long after she was removed from power.

To her doe-eyed, unwavering supporters, she will always be Maggie. Maggie, Maggie, Maggie (sigh). To the left she is Thatcher. Thatcher who progressed from simple milk snatcher to union basher.

She had seen her Tory predecessor, Edward Heath, humiliated by the unions while the Labour governments of Harold Wilson and Jim Callaghan were treated with contempt. So Thatcher plotted the emasculation of the unions with stealth and cunning.

When she came to power in 1979 she moved slowly at first with her grand plan to marginalise the unions. The Employment Acts of 1980 and 1982 outlawed secondary strike action and flying pickets. It wasn't until she had won the Falklands War and been re-elected in 1983 that she ratcheted up her attack. Over the next few years, the closed shop was banned, secret ballots for union elections were made compulsory, unions were made legally responsible for unofficial actions by their members and employers were given the right to sack unofficial strikers.

The screw was further tightened after Thatcher became emboldened by the defeat of the miners. Seven days' notice of a strike had to be given (making the instant walk-out illegal), ballots for industrial action were more tightly regulated and employees given the right to join a union of their choice (allowing maverick little unions to sprout up and undermine the major ones). It was a very one-sided war, with the unions losing power, influence and millions of members along with most of their rights.

The balance of power shifted back to the employers and the union barons were left high and dry like whales on a beach when the tide has gone out.

# Hate figures 2: fat cats in flat caps

Once upon a time, union leaders were almost as well known as footballers. In the 1970s it often seemed as though more people were on strike than at work and union leaders were on TV and in the papers as much as Noel Edmonds.

They were the Atomic Kittens of their day – all of a kind. Union leaders were middle-aged or elderly men, some of them stridently left wing (even former commu-nists, which sent sections of the media into hysterics) while others were simply stuck in reactionary old ways. Most had impenetrable accents – at least, impenetrable to people who lived south of Watford, which made them even more terrifying to the London press. These were the union 'barons' and the unions were their fiefdoms, stretching across great swathes of British industry from docks and railways to car plants and factories. As unions grew and became more powerful so did the people running them, even if they had started out as an electrician, postman, fitter or machine operator.

They also became terribly rich – the fat cats of socialism. At least, they did if you want to believe the right-wing propaganda machine. The Taxpayers' Alliance – a self-appointed pressure group devoted to showing that every penny raised in tax is misspent, even if it is on saving the lives of children or caring for the housebound elderly – has made union leaders a particular target. (Why? What taxpayers' money do they get?)

Anyway, according to the TA, there are no less than THIRTY-EIGHT union general secretaries and chief executives who are paid more than £100,000 a year. A HUNDRED GRAND. *How obscene!* How utterly disgraceful! They are just ripping off their members, aren't they? Actually, no. It just isn't true that there are thirty-eight union chiefs earning that much. In fact, at the last count there were two, one of whom runs the teachers' union.

The truth is that the people who lead unions, while certainly earning more than their members, which you would except in a socialist paradise, on the whole get modestly paid for what they do.

Derek Simpson and Tony Woodley, the joint general secretaries of the newly united Unite, each earn around £60,000 a year, for running an organisation with almost two million members and an annual income of more than

£200 million. Can the Taxpayers' Alliance point to a single boss in the commercial world who would take on such responsibility for such little reward? Thought not.

It is true that union leaders do have perks. Derek Simpson is said to have negotiated a 'house for life' as part of his package. While Andy Gilchrist, leader of the firemen's union, ran up an £817.31 bill at a posh Indian restaurant just a poppadom's throw from the House of Commons. In case you were wondering, Mr Gilchrist wasn't entertaining the entire FBU membership – just four members of his executive.

Unions own property, employ thousands of people ranging from lawyers to organisers, archivists and press officers and have financial interests in pension funds and other investments. They have become an industry in themselves.

Yet their leaders remain hate figures. They will proudly appear at a union conference or seminar but do they admit what they do when they are on holiday with their families or out for the evening with the wife? Highly unlikely. Why would they want to put themselves through the sneering or abuse which may follow?

Even the union bosses who have no direct reputation as militants and troublemakers are tarred by association with those who are.

Threadbare footnote: not all union chiefs earn this sort

of money. The leader of the National Union of Flint Glass-workers gets a paltry £1,750 a year. What skinflints his executive must be.

# Mr Gordon Taylor: an interlude

There is one union leader who does earn rather a lot. He is Gordon Taylor and a few years ago he became the first employee of a union whose salary topped a million pounds. Good, eh?

However, his union does not represent low-paid workers whose hard-earned pennies are torn from their grasp to fund his high-living existence on a tropical island. Gordon Taylor is the general secretary of the Professional Footballers' Association, so he is actually one of the few leaders of a union whose members earn more than him. Some pick up getting on for a million pounds a month. They probably think of Mr Taylor's income as close to the poverty line.

It is certainly a far cry from his early days. He started his working life as an apprentice for Bolton Wanderers, getting just £12 a week. In those days he was a promising schoolboy who played on the wing. So Gordon Taylor is not merely the only union leader who is a millionaire, he is the only one who is neither a left-winger nor a right-winger, but simply a winger.

# Mr Adam Crozier: another interlude

It's hard work being a boss, but someone's got to do it. All that battling against the odds for scant reward with the constant risk of being kicked out with nothing if you don't make the grade.

At least, that is the whining argument propounded by the boss class.

These titans of the business world may have what seem to be massive salaries and bonuses (at least, they look massive to anyone not earning them) but, their supporters insist, they are a select group of brilliant businessmen whose value to an organisation is incalculable. True or not true?

To help you decide, let us look at just one example of this remarkable group. Consider the case of Mr Adam Crozier. He was an advertising man who suddenly, at the age of thirty-five, was propelled into running the Football Association, even though he had little experience of running anything and his main contact with football had been when he had a trial with Stirling Albion. His reign at the FA was understandably much criticised.

However, that didn't stop him then being put in charge of the Royal Mail, one of this country's proudest and most important institutions. At least, it was before he got his hands on it. The Crozier years were marked by a worsening of the service, industrial unrest and large increases in the price of posting letters.

If you think this means it was the end of Crozier's career, you haven't been following the plot. His efforts were rewarded with enormous bonuses on top of his gigantic salary. And then he was head-hunted for *another* big job with an even bigger salary and even bigger bonuses.

In his final year as chief executive of the Royal Mail, Crozier picked up a pay packet of £2.43 million, which included a bonus of £1.57 million, even though the company had failed to hit its targets. This boss's income was 105 times larger than that of a postman. And he didn't have to start work at five o'clock in the morning and trudge the streets in rain, snow and blazing sun.

Hang on a minute. Are we being a bit harsh? After all, Crozier did preside over Royal Mail's profits increasing, so he must be a genius and worth all that money, mustn't he?

That is the story peddled by the City, management consultants and bosses' mates in politics and the media. They want to persuade workers to excuse the obscene sums paid to bosses by making them believe that being a successful captain of industry is a really skilful occupation.

You don't need to go to some expensive management school to learn how to do it. We can explain briefly, simply and for no extra charge (this book really is exceptionally good value for money). This is how to be a profit-boosting boss, a plan worked with remarkable success not just by Adam Crozier but hundreds like him.

First, you sack lots of workers. Doesn't matter how long they have worked for the firm, how loyal they have been, how difficult it will be for them to get another job. Get rid of them. Out the door. Done? Right, that's brought down the costs of running the company, hasn't it?

Now make the remaining employees work longer hours for the same money. This is known as increased efficiency. Getting a lot more out of fewer workers. What do you mean, they never get home to see their kids now and some of them fall ill with the pressure? Do they want a job or not? If they don't, there are plenty willing to take their place (we know that because we sacked them and they are still on the dole).

The next step is to hold down wages. You have to do that because the organisation is in such dire straits that pay rises would send it to the wall. Not all wages need to be pegged, though. There is some room for flexibility. So your own salary and those of other directors and senior managers can go soaring without the slightest threat to the future of the firm.

Finally, you put up your prices. As high as you can get away with. Some customers may moan but to hell with them. They can't go anywhere else for a stamp, for example.

This is the way most (not all, let's be fair) bosses behaved and they were only resisted when the unions became strong and the workers, on the whole, managed to defend their incomes and their rights. But then came the Thatcher anti-union laws to swing the balance of power back in favour of the employers and the old management styles returned where they could. As long as there are bosses like this around, who says there is no place for unions?

PS. Adam Crozier has left Royal Mail and is now running ITV, despite knowing little about television beyond how to switch on his set. Though he could afford to pay someone to do that for him – he is expected to earn £14 million over the next five years.

# The way of the working world

This is the story of two men. They might have been born in the same hospital at the same time, but they weren't. They might have gone to the same school and had the same educational advantages, but they didn't. They might live next door to each other, but they don't. What they do have in common is that they work for the same company.

One is the chief executive of this firm, Mr B (for Boss).

He earns £200,000 a year but it's not enough to keep him in the manner to which he insists on being accustomed or to properly reward him for the very special contribution he makes and the brilliance he brings to the company (though, admittedly, its share price has halved in the past two years and profits have dropped dramatically). So he has been awarded an extra £100,000 a year as a bonus (that's in a bad year; in a good year, if there is one, he can expect several times more than that). Plus he gets a generous wodge of shares every so often. Plus he has a luxurious car, paid for by the firm. Plus generous expenses, which include always flying business class (after all, he is a businessman, as he points out with a chuckle). Plus a very generous pension which is worth several million pounds and will provide him with an income well above six figures when he retires at the age of fifty-two, exhausted by his gruelling life. Plus a little flat for him to stay in when he is too bushed to struggle home at the end of the working day. Plus an annual pay rise that has averaged 10 per cent over the past five years.

Then there is the minus. No, not a minus for him, a minus for the taxman. For, thanks to a *terrific* accountant he was recommended to by another boss, Mr B manages to avoid paying tax on much of his income.

Now let us look at the other person employed by this

company. He is Mr W, (for Worker, naturally – wake up at the back). He is at work by 8 a.m. every day and is never away before six. He gets only a short lunch break and the pressure on him is relentless. He has been doing this job for fifteen years and earns something short of twenty grand a year. He does his job conscientiously, never takes time off with a sickie and gets four weeks' holiday a year, two of which he spends in Spain on a cheap package. Everything he earns is taxed at source, so, with tax and national insurance taken off, he is giving the state around 25 per cent of his income.

Now, let's see if you have been paying attention. Because Mr W has been around so long and is considered by his colleagues to be reliable and trustworthy, he has become a union official in the local branch. And, as the workers have been pegged to a 2 per cent pay rise for the third year in a row despite being expected to cover for a number of their co-workers who were made redundant, he helps to organise a ballot of union members to see if they want to take industrial action.

Now here's the question: one of these two men is denounced as a threat to society, a menace who could bring the entire edifice of Britain crashing to the ground. A greedy, grasping individual who cares only for himself. In the best style of *Blind Date*, you have to decide which of these men it is. Is it:

★ Mr B, who is ripping off shareholders, employees and taxpayers? *Or*

★ Mr W, who is doing his job conscientiously for scant reward and trying to get a bit more for his colleagues?

Yes, that's right. It is Mr W. He and workers like him are the traitors who threaten this country's prosperity and stability, and who are regularly denounced by the press, politicians and members of the establishment. Their crime is to dare to ask for a bit more – just as Oliver Twist's was – while the fat cats get away with ripping off the nation without criticism or censure. Even the Great Banking Scandal hasn't changed that.

As the Bible puts it so eloquently: To them that have, let more be given. To them that have not, they shall receive a bucket of shit from the *Daily Mail*.

# Genesis of the unions

In the beginning, there was work. Well, there was God's work. And since He did it all on His own, He didn't need to belong to a union.

Admittedly he worked incredibly hard, but he was his own boss so organised the massive task of creating the universe so he could have Sunday off (actually, it was probably Saturday, but let's not get into a theological argument; there's enough else to squabble about).

If we had all continued to do our own thing, like Adam and Cain, tilling our own little bit of land to provide just what we needed, there would never have been economic inequality. After all, if you are self-employed, you are not going to storm in to see yourself and demand a pay rise or to work fewer hours, let alone threaten yourself that you will go on strike if your demands aren't met.

But the world moved on, even though there still weren't any unions when the workers were slaves or serfs. For a crucial requisite for the creation of unions is that there should be a free relationship between the bosses and the workers. Well, free-ish. With the attitude of much of the employer class, aided and abetted by politicians, there never will be a genuinely free relationship this side of heaven.

The existence of unions is a formalisation of the right to say we won't be dictated to. You could say that the Greek women who refused to have sex with their husbands until they ended the Peloponnesian War (around 400BC) were in a kind of trade union, with the indomitable Lysistrata as their shop steward as she organised them to withhold their favours, if not their labours. (Homework: can having sex with your husband ever be described as a trade? Discuss.)

You might even say that the aristocrats who confronted

The sex strike by Greek women in 400BC is resolved to everyone's satisfaction.

King John at Runnymede in 1215 and forced him to sign Magna Carta were a short-lived union (The National Union of Lords, Knights and Pissed-Off Aristos?). They got together for a common purpose and took action against a common antagonist, forcing him to come to an agreement by united action. Unfortunately, their heirs have been downtreading servants and employees for the succeeding 800 years.

Sporadic actions such as these proved that people are stronger when they organise together for a common purpose. Bosses of all kinds, from kings down, understand that only too well. This is why they cracked down hard on the slightest sign of workers combining together.

# Long ago and Pharaoh way

Most people think official union militancy has a history that doesn't stretch much further back than a century. Wrong, wrong, wrong.

The first known strike was on 14 November 1170BC, in Egypt during the reign of Pharaoh Rameses III. That is a long time ago even by the standards of the Labour movement, yet there are amazing resonances with modern industrial disputes.

It began when there was a drought leading to the crops failing, which pushed up the price of grain sharply, though the cost of slaves remained constant, you will be delighted to hear.

This meant Rameses was unable to provide enough rations for his elite tomb builders, who were the key workers of the day, although their profession has fallen into disuse over the ensuing centuries. Slaves continued to be fed (they didn't need much, after all). So the tomb builders withdrew their labour.

Thus this dispute was about workers demanding more because of steeply rising inflation and what was considered to be favourable treatment accorded to cheap immigrant labour (slaves being about as cheap as immigrant labour can get).

Those of us who lived through the so-called 'Winter of

Discontent' (see pages 101–3) will remember the hysterical newspaper headline 'Now they won't even let us bury our dead'. How remarkable that Rameses III will have been saying precisely the same about the strike of the tomb builders 3,131 years earlier.

The reason we know about this strike in ancient Egypt is that it was faithfully recorded in detail on papyrus, the *Daily Mail* not being published at the time.

There continued to be outbreaks of workers' militancy down the centuries but it wasn't until the Industrial Revolution that strikes came into their own. After all, you can't have proper industrial disputes without proper industries. And tomb-building, though an important industry at the time, died out with the Pharaohs.

From these quite early times, there was a clear division between the attitudes of bosses and workers to work. Workers did it because they needed to, originally to earn enough to pay for the basics of life; later, to earn enough to pay for some of its little luxuries. Bosses work because it gives them power, it gives them influence and it gives them lots of money and the promise of even more. Some work quite hard, admittedly. Some even work exceptionally hard. But some do bugger all, swanning about on the golf course or on their yacht or in the villa they have had built in the Bahamas, from where they mock the 'wage slaves' back home.

41

Quite a lot of new 'jobs' have been created to take advantage of the opportunities that arise because ordinary workers have more money than in previous generations. This is a modern version of the conmen who turned up every pay day to persuade the hard workers to part with their money easily. In the same way, there are slick people today who sell workers things they don't need and usually don't really want, but can be persuaded that they do. Sometimes they extract their money for 'investments' which make a fortune only for the people who sell them.

# TIGMOO: yet another interlude

No group of people more enjoys wallowing in tradition than trade unionists. At times their love of the movement sinks into sentimentality tinged with cliché. And there is no cliché they love more than This Great Movement of Ours, incomprehensibly shortened to Tigmoo.

Even if we concede that there have been some great things about the union movement, so have there been about all sorts of other organisations. Yet no one at John Lewis or the Home Office or the Boy Scouts talks about This Great Movement of Ours.

Many trade unionists, particularly of a certain age, can't get to their feet without letting the phrase slip from their lips. In fact, the expression 'the movement' has come to be used in only two connections, one being unions and the other bowels.

Sadly, in the way of things in the modern world, even this famous phrase has been shortened to the acronym Tigmoo, which has in turn become the name of a new website.* How the founders of This Great Movement of Ours must be turning in their graves now that their favourite cliché has come to sound like the title of a show for the under-fives on CBeebies: 'Hi there, kids. How are you tigmoo-ing today? Tiggy the cow has been having a lovely time ringing her new bell. . .' And so on.

Such shallowness (though, admittedly, three-year-olds don't expect Dostoevsky) is in sharp contrast to the proper use of Tigmoo – sorry, This Great Movement of Ours – when orators attempt to drag in the achievements of long-ago battles in support of the struggles of today.

This doesn't often bear close examination. An industrial dispute over some minor contractual point or an increased pay rise is not going to figure in the pantheons of Labour history. So what is the point of summoning up the spirit of This Great Movement of Ours?

But that is the point, as far as the official who is Tigmoo-ing is concerned. Every dispute is as important as any

---

* If you want to have a look at the website, you can find it at http://www.tigmoo.co.uk. It's rather good, actually.

other. Each one is another step on the long, winding road that is This Great Movement of Ours.

There was a time when it worked. When members did get fired up by identifying their own, sometimes puny, problems with the great, historic battles of the past. Does it still rouse them? Unlikely. And relegating This Great Movement of Ours to a Tigmoo seems to confirm it.

# Good news! Millions dead!

The history of trade unions is a catalogue of attempts to ban them, neuter them, criminalise their members and persecute their leaders. Any excuse would do. In the middle of the fourteenth century, King Edward III used the pretence of the Black Death. He outlawed unions and collective bargaining by passing The Ordinance of Labourers (1349).

The Black Death, by killing around 40 per cent of the population, had wiped out a sizeable chunk of the workforce. Displaying the sort of thinking which became common among political forces in league with bosses down the succeeding 700 years, Edward claimed that the shortage of labour would mean that workers could charge more for their labour. Shameful! So landowners would be faced with either paying higher wages or leaving their land unused.

Higher pay for labourers meant goods became more expensive to produce and the wealthy landowners would see their profits hit. Sound familiar? So the obvious thing to do was force the workers to stay on the same wages.

There would be no saying to young Jimmy: 'I'm so sorry your father, brothers and uncles have died a horrible death, leaving you to care for the rest of your family – you must have more money.' Instead it was: 'Don't think you're getting more just because of the good fortune of the Black Death.'

The Law of Ordinance stated:

- ★ Everyone under sixty must work
- ★ Employers must not hire excess workers
- ★ Employers may not pay and workers may not receive wages higher than pre-plague levels
- ★ Food must be priced reasonably with no excess profit.

Most crucial from our point of view was that it made illegal any attempt on the part of workers to bargain collectively. How long do you think this compassionate piece of legislation stayed on the statute books? Repealed as soon as the population levels picked up? Not at all. It remained law for 514 years – that is *five hundred and fourteen* – until it was scrapped in 1863, by which time the country had been through another period of huge change, the Industrial Revolution.

# Trouble at t'mill

If you were paying attention at school when this bit came up in history, you'll know that between the late eighteenth and mid-nineteenth centuries, Britain changed from a largely rural society into one in which industrial production made possible by the new power sources – steam and coal – was the driver for wealth creation. Places like Manchester and Leeds, which had been villages less than a century earlier, expanded rapidly as stagecoaches became able to reach them in mere days thanks to the opening of the M6.

Factories were built to house the new machines and the workforce suddenly included women, children, rural workers and immigrants (mainly Irish in those days). This new pool of unskilled and semi-skilled labour was one of the starting points for the development of unions. Political radicalism was growing. There were pamphlets and protests against the 'tax on knowledge', a duty imposed on newspapers which priced them out of the reach of the poor. (Abolition of this tax on knowledge has allowed the publication of important political organs such as the *Daily Star* and *Daily Sport*.) The aristocracy remained the ruling class, with a new breed of industrialists coming through, while fewer than half a million men (no women, of course) had the right to vote.

Many different workers' organisations sprang up – co-operatives, friendly societies and labour exchanges, most of them concerned with protecting and improving workers' living standards, but there were others which were to become a force for changing the political and social order of Britain.

# Give us a break

By the start of the nineteenth century, workers in the textile industry had developed a new sport – smashing looms and any other piece of new machinery they could lay their hands, hammers or axes on. They saw these mechanised processes as a threat to their livelihoods.

The wreckers were known as Luddites, taking their name from the original smasher, who variously took the titles King Ludd, General Ludd and Captain Ludd, although the original Ludd was called, simply, Ned. The authorities reacted sharply, particularly when the Luddites formed themselves into a fighting force and did battle with the mighty British army.

Many of them were rounded up, arrested and put on

trial. Some were sent to Australia for penal servitude while others were executed. Even Mrs Thatcher didn't react as strongly as that.

# It don't mean a thing if it ain't Captain Swing

Captain Swing was not some snake-hipped crooner popular in working men's clubs in the 1830s but a furious letter writer. Although he probably didn't exist as a real person, threatening letters signed 'Captain Swing' were sent to magistrates, landowners, farmers and clergymen protesting at the introduction of new threshing machines which would put many farm labourers out of work. The so-called Swing Rioters, whose slogan was 'Bread Not Blood', went on the rampage, smashing up the new machines, burning hayricks and wrecking tithe barns and workhouses.

It was a well-organised campaign of industrial action which spread across the country and created a deadly enemy in the shape of the Home Secretary, Lord Melbourne, who had recently introduced a number of anti-union laws. He not only had no sympathy for the farm workers, he wanted to punish them. Hundreds were arrested, nine were hanged and 450 sentenced to be deported to Australia.

To make matters worse, the government decided the way to deal with the growing number of poor and unemployed was to make the workhouses as vile as possible to discourage the lazy scroungers from going there. Families were split up, conditions in the workhouses were appal-ling and poverty was rife. Out of this misery and social unrest grew a new political party. Enter the Chartists.

# Top of the Charters

In 1848, two million people signed a Charter making six demands. They may sound rather familiar 162 years later. They were:

1. A VOTE for every man of twenty-one years of age, of sound mind and not undergoing punishment for crime.
2. A SECRET BALLOT
3. NO PROPERTY QUALIFICATION for Members of Parliament, so anyone could stand as an MP (there was no mention of second homes or duck houses at this stage).
4. MPS TO BE PAID, so any ordinary 'tradesman, working man or other person can serve a constituency,

when taken from his business to attend to the interests of the Country'.

5. EQUAL CONSTITUENCIES, securing the same amount of representation for the same number of electors, instead of allowing small constituencies to swamp the votes of large ones. (This same proposal has just been described by Labour Shadow Justice Secretary Jack Straw as deeply undemocratic and gerrymandering.)

6. ANNUAL PARLIAMENTS 'thus presenting the most effectual check to bribery and intimidation, since though a constituency might be bought once in seven years, no purse could buy a constituency in each ensuing twelve-month; and since members, when elected for a year only, would not be able to defy and betray their constituents as now.'

Despite the phenomenal support for these proposals, the leaders, known as Chartists, were arrested while trying to march to Westminster to deliver them. One of the Chartists was William Cuffay, a black tailor and son of a slave. Cuffay was tried for 'levying war against the Queen' and sentenced to transportation for life to Van Diemen's Land, now Tasmania. So no institutional racism there, then.

The industrialists of the time showed their sympathy for the Chartists' demands by cutting the wages of workers in the cotton industry by 25 per cent. The Chartists began to squabble among themselves and their great, noble cause fizzled out, pending the time when Liberal Democrats might form part of a coalition government.

# An everyday story of country folk

Nowadays a lot of fuss is made about swearing. You are always reading how outraged and shocked viewers are at the amount of swearing on television. Disgraceful what Russell Brand gets away with, isn't it? But in 1834, the authorities were concerned about a different kind of swearing – the taking of an oath by workers to stay loyal to each other when they together tried to get higher wages.

On 24 February 1834, six farm labourers from Tolpuddle, in Dorset, were arrested on a charge of taking part in an 'illegal oath' ceremony. They had dared to form a union – the Friendly Society of Agricultural Labourers – to defend their livelihood. They refused to work for less than ten shillings (50p) a week, their wages having been slashed to seven shillings with another cut to six shillings (30p) coming (George Osborne must have been running the farming industry).

For this heinous crime, the Tolpuddle Six were sentenced to seven years' transportation to the penal colonies of Australia. (A bit different to the penalty for swearing on TV today – Russell Brand only got deported to Hollywood.)

As news of the sentence spread (remember, no Twitter or Facebook then), the fledgling trade union movement began organising a campaign for their release. A month after the arrests, there was a Grand Meeting of the Working Classes, called by the Grand National Consolidated Trades Union and attended by more than 10,000 people. Agitation and anger spread and the London Central Dorchester Committee was formed to campaign to have the men pardoned.

On 21 April some 100,000 people gathered in Copenhagen Fields near King's Cross. The government feared disorder. Even by Mrs Thatcher's standards they went rather over the top with their precautions. The Life Guards (obviously not the beach type), the Household Troop, detachments of lancers, two troops of dragoons, eight battalions of infantry and twenty-nine pieces of ordnance or cannon were mustered. More than 5,000 special constables were sworn in and the city looked like an armed camp. Which it was.

With banners flying, the grand procession marched to Parliament cheered on by spectators lining the streets and perched on roof tops. At Whitehall the petition was taken to the office of the Home Secretary, Lord Melbourne, who hid behind his curtains and refused to accept it (as recorded by the Sky News helicopter hovering overhead).

The government did all it could to resist the mounting protest. Radical MPs such as William Cobbett, Joseph Hume and Thomas Wakley kept raising the question in the Commons and petitions containing more than 800,000 signatures came from all over the country, a remarkable achievement when there was not only no internet but a low level of literacy (the petitions wouldn't have been as impressive if they had contained 800,000 crosses).

By June 1835, ten months after the men had arrived in Australia, conditional pardons were granted. But that was not good enough and the pressure continued until the government agreed on 14 March the following year that all the men should have a full and free pardon and return home, which they did after watching England thrash the Aussies in the Test matches that summer.

To this day, the Tolpuddle Martyrs are hailed as the first major victory for the union movement in this country and are celebrated at an annual festival in Dorset. While Lord Melbourne, the self-styled scourge of trade unions, is recalled as the man who hid behind the curtains when the marchers came but not when his wife was shagging Lord Byron.

# Strike a light OR Light a strike

A strike by a couple of hundred skinny girls, some just thirteen years old, did more for the union movement in the late 1880s than any belligerent blokes around at the time. The girls were employed by the Bryant & May match company in London's East End. Forced to work in appallingly dirty and dangerous conditions, standing for twelve hours each day, they were paid a pittance. The socialist campaigner Annie Besant published an account of the dreadful way the girls were treated in a paper called *The Link*.

Bryant & May bosses dismissed the report as 'twaddle' and sacked one of the girls, who they accused of being the ringleader who had provided the information for the article. These poor, uneducated and unskilled young women refused to be treated as liars and downed tools, marching to *The Link*'s Fleet Street office. It was a public relations disaster for Bryant & May, decades before anyone had heard of public relations. Annie Besant helped to organise a strike fund and there was mass support for the match girls. Bryant & May caved in and the girls returned to work victorious in their battle for better pay and conditions.

Not only had they won their fight, they had found public sympathy and a supportive newspaper, and sparked a new awareness among the unskilled working class. Within a year, the Gas Workers and General Labourers' Union was formed and won an eight-hour day. This was followed by a 60,000-strong dockers' strike which virtually closed a stretch of the Thames for over a month.

The workers had found their voice and their power. And it was all down to those sparky little match girls.


# Rise and fall

Question: how many unions are there? Answer: nothing like as many as there used to be.

At one time, as well as the giants which dominated the TUC and the headlines, there was a plethora of small unions, some really tiny. They sprang up to represent groups of workers in a particular but limited industry or those who had certain skills.

For many years the Jewish Bakers' Union was a particular favourite of left-wing Trivial Pursuit players, with its eleven members making it the smallest union in the country (sad they couldn't even get a dozen, let alone a baker's dozen). Even recruitment drives among bagel makers couldn't save it in a world where size mattered and eventually it was wound up, its remaining members presumably seeking a home with the gentiles of the Bakers, Food and Allied Workers Union.

JO PHILLIPS & DAVID SEYMOUR

A glance at the unions which have ceased to exist in the past few years gives a nostalgic insight into a world that used to be. Let us wave a fond farewell to the Associated Chiropodists and Podiatrists Union. To the Church and Oswaldtwistle Power-Loom Overlookers Association. To the Ice Hockey Players' Association (Great Britain). The Society of Registration Officers (Births, Deaths and Marriages). And the Union of the Federation of Employed Door Supervisors and Security.

Not all is lost for their members, though. Some defunct unions become part of a larger one, although with a less romantic name. So anyone who enjoys working with feet can now belong to the Society of Chiropractors and Podiatrists (which must have dropped the word 'union' from its title to appear more upmarket) while bouncers can join the snappily named Door Supervisors Union.

Some unions which pass into history have a great past and their passing is mourned by Labour movement sentimentalists. Those who remember with affection the great years of union power find it hard to believe that the Transport and General Workers' Union is no more. It merged with Amicus to create Unite. Amicus itself was the result of a merger between the AEEU (Amalgamated Electrical and Engineering Union) and the MSF (Manufacturing, Science and Finance).

What has been lost by the creation of these new super-unions is the sense of industrial identity that came with the old structure. The AEEU was the organisation which represented the elite skilled manual workers, and rather unpopular they were at times with their brethren from other, more general, unions.

The MSF was a brilliant creation, led by the mercurial Welshman Clive Jenkins for many years. He spotted the opportunity of expanding white-collar trade unionism and took the MSF from a minor organisation to one of the big hitters.

Today there are around 175 registered unions, though some are just regions of larger organisations while others can hardly be described as industrial behemoths – Aegis the Union, for example, and the Harrods Staff Union. The number actually affiliated to the TUC is around sixty.

Astonishingly, however, this is roughly only half the number of employers' associations, which are organisations formed by companies to deal collectively with workers and unions in their particular industrial or commercial areas.

It is one of the ironies of life that whereas trade unions have been subject to endless attacks on their ability to effectively represent their members, employers' associations can pretty well do what they like. Of course. The stronger they are, the more they can do down the workers. So that's all right, then.

# Meet the activists

In most walks of life it is a compliment to say someone is an activist. As in: 'She is still active even though she is nearly ninety' or 'He is very active in the village, helping to organise the annual fete and running the allotments.'

There is only one instance in which calling someone an activist is a term of abuse. And that is when they are active in a union.

To say someone is a union activist implies he is a revolutionary whose every waking moment is dedicated to destroying the company he works for en route to bringing down the government before moving on to wreck society.

This is a strange use of language and has only taken hold because the media and political establishment want workers – and particularly trade unionists – to be passive. Not *pacifists*, though, as that suggests they are lily-livered individuals who won't fight for their country. Fighting for your country is good; fighting for your rights at work and colleagues is *bad*.

Activists, as their name implies, are the backbone of any union organisation. Without them, their work, their dedication to endless long and boring meetings, collecting subscriptions and maintaining the basic structure of the organisation, there would be no unions.

It is a convenient fiction for the above-mentioned media

and political establishment to portray union members as two distinct breeds. There are the activists, who are nothing but trouble, and the rest, who would rather spend their time feeding the goldfish or trimming the lawn in their neat back garden than get involved in union activity.

It isn't that easy to pigeon-hole them. At times, like Dr Jekyll becoming Mr Hyde, those mild-mannered passive union members rise up and become active, throwing out a 'generous' 1 per cent pay offer, for example, or even threatening to strike.

Shame on them! How can normally gentle, ostensibly easy-going folk change like that? Simple, according to the conspiracy theorists in the – yes, you've got it – media and political establishment. *They have been brain-washed by the activists!*

Of course. Under normal circumstances, those mild members would have been quite happy to accept whatever grossly insulting droppings the bosses offered as a pay rise or working conditions.

# Division of labour

Imagine this scenario. You have finished your family Sunday lunch and it's time to clear up. You ask Jane to take the plates into the kitchen. She goes to pick one up but Jim, her brother, stops her and says that is his job. She has to take out the knives and forks, he insists. Then Simon, their cousin, leaps in to say no, she only takes the forks; he is responsible for the knives.

Out in the kitchen, Aunty Sally is about to load the plates into the dishwasher but Uncle Harry gets cross with her (he did drink two glasses of wine) and says that is his job. She can only load the soup bowls. Granny is sent to Coventry because she stacked the glasses and it is a family tradition that you do that. She is only allowed to carry out the empty vegetable dishes – although the meat plate is the province of Grandad.

How crazy does that sound? Yet it is only a partially exaggerated version of what used to go on in factories throughout Britain.

Different unions – and even members of the same union – had sharply defined roles at work and were strictly forbidden from straying into any other job. That meant one lot of workers putting the wheels on a car and another doing up the nuts. Or one group being restricted to doing maintenance on metal objects while another could only do wood and yet another anything paper related.

In really OTT union situations, although one group had to perform a particular task, another would have to be present. Sometimes more than one. A small office could be full of men standing watching while the jammed lock (metal) on a (wooden) filing cabinet was sorted out (a maintenance task, but they could only watch, not touch metal – or wood).

There is obviously sense in not letting someone loose on a job for which he hasn't been trained. Do you want the hospital porter to operate on you? But demarcation disputes weren't about efficiency, competence or potential danger. They were about preserving very narrow job roles for particular groups of workers.

With sickening regularity, these battle lines would flare up into some totally needless stand-off, with management confronted with an ultimatum and walk-outs threatened and often happening. These were demarcation disputes and British industry was infested with them. 'Who does what' rows were a major symbol of what became known as 'the British disease'.

By reducing productivity drastically, artificial demarcation, ruthlessly enforced, was bad for industry and the economy. It was also unfair on large numbers of workers, who were capable of doing certain jobs but denied the opportunity because they weren't in the right union or even the right section of their own union.

Demarcations, and particularly demarcation disputes, have all but vanished from the scene. There are two main reasons for this. One is the decline in industry and particularly the sharp fall in union membership in the private sector. The other is that modern ways of working, particularly now so much is computerised and high-tech, have made the old artificial barriers obsolete.

# Don't be left behind, all right?

The way union members and particularly their leaders are presented in the press, you could be forgiven for thinking that they were all wild-eyed left-wing revolutionaries committed to bringing down the state and declaring a socialist republic.

While it is true that there are a few like that, they are tiny in number. Ultra-left politics has never caught on in this country, even if 0.00000001 per cent of the population still dream the dream.

The political views of the vast majority of union members are little different from those of non-members. They are on the whole more likely to vote Labour than Conservative but there are an awful lot who find no inconsistency with belonging to a union and supporting the Tories. In fact, Mrs Thatcher attracted the votes of a great number, despite doing all she could to undermine the unions. That might not make sense, but we are dealing with people and politics here. If you want sense and logic, join the Magic Circle.

While there are unlikely to be any senior union officials who go so far as to support the Conservatives, there is a long history of what the left call right-wing union leaders. What they mean is not that they are in the BNP but they are somewhere equally repellent to them, on the right of the Labour Party.

Though this makes them outcasts in the eyes of the left, they have often more accurately reflected the views of their members, most of whom are more interested in getting on with life rather than being involved in permanent political upheaval.

Most union leaders don't want to lead the revolution; they want to be part of the existing system. This isn't because they are desperate for an easy life, home by five o'clock every night with their slippers by the fire and tea on the table, but because it is the best way to achieve things for their members.

Bosses – and politicians – are more likely to come to a deal with people who don't seem hell bent on confrontation (see 'You *can* always get what you want' on pages 125–30). That doesn't mean right-wing union officials are a push-over. The reputations of some of those most hated by the left for their 'soft' political views are as the toughest bargainers. Having an underlying political agenda isn't going to make you the greatest negotiator. Members of the jury, I call in evidence Mr Arthur Scargill.

# The TUC

The 1860s weren't a good time for the embryo trade unions. A nasty court judgment had deprived them of protection of their funds so employers or third parties could sue if they were affected by a strike. The press (not the *Daily Mail*, though, which wasn't founded for another thirty-five years) had denounced them for unpatriotically undermining Britain's trade position in the face of low-wage competition from abroad. Bosses in Sheffield and elsewhere had developed the lock-out (see 'The reverse strike: a cunning trick' on pages 103–5), to subvert the unions and bring workers to heel.

To cap it all, the government appointed a royal commission to inquire into the unions, pretending it was all Queen Victoria's idea in grief at the death of Prince Albert. There was a real fear that it would return with proposals that would turn back the clock to 1824, when all trade combinations had been illegal.

As if this wasn't worrying enough, bosses were picking off unions one by one as individually they weren't big enough or had the resources to fight back effectively. Co-ordinating information, let alone action, was painfully slow and difficult in those days.

So was born the idea that every year the unions should gather together in a huge meeting. So huge, in fact, that they would call it a congress. The Trades Union Congress.

Thus was created the fledgling TUC, which is still the organisation that provides the umbrella for unions. It has been able to settle disputes between unions (or not, as the case may be, but at least it has tried) as well as deal with the government of the day and agree on united policy from not a handful or even a few thousand trade unionists, but millions of them. That makes it one of the most powerful voices in the country.

The TUC has been pivotal in pressing the great demands for political and industrial reform, ranging from stopping young children working and getting the vote for working men to the introduction of maternity and paternity leave and the minimum wage.

However, it has never been smooth sailing. If there were a poll to identify the worst job of the twentieth century, being general secretary of the TUC would surely come near the top. Especially when the union barons were immensely powerful and the loathing between them verged on venomous. Brotherly love? No, brotherly hatred was the principal emotion. It went on throughout the year but the week of the annual Congress was unremitting plotting and intrigue, tinged at times with farce.

Unions really mattered in those days so the Labour Party leadership trembled with fear at what they would do and say, for their decisions could in theory commit the party to some outrageous policy or course of action which would drive away voters in droves. Strictly speaking, if the TUC decided something must be done – for example, all workers should have their pay doubled or be given six months' holiday or the country should join a new Common Market with Cuba and North Korea – that proposal would carry on to the Labour conference, where the union block vote could then make it party policy.

Leading Labour politicians and TUC chiefs spent ridiculous amounts of time and effort desperately trying to tone down the more extraordinary proposals. What went on in those famed 'smoke-filled rooms' was beyond the imagination of anyone who hasn't experienced union plotting at its most labyrinthine.

The result of a particular debate would hinge on which way one of the big unions voted. So that union's executive would hole up in their seaside hotel, arguing, arguing, arguing, and trying to persuade the other members to go with them. If there were, say, thirty-one people on an executive, it only needed sixteen of them for a majority that would swing the vote which committed that union to cast its entire block vote that way at the conference. So those sixteen delegates ended up being able to throw in a million or more conference votes. Great thing, democracy, isn't it?

The peak of absurdity – so incredibly bonkers that it even shocked hardened union watchers – was when a union voted both ways. This really happened on a few crucial issues. The chairman of Congress would ask 'All those in favour' and big union X would cast its million votes. These tipped the balance in favour of the motion. Or did they? For when the chairman asked 'All those against' union X voted again, cancelling out its previous million votes, swinging the balance the other way and defeating the motion. How this came about was that the general secretary or president, who had the union's voting card firmly in his hand, didn't like the way they had voted. So he cast what were in effect his personal million votes the other way. This lunacy was allowed to stand because the rules didn't say you couldn't vote for and against the same motion. (Why should they? You'd have to be mad to think anyone would do that.)

And the unions wondered why they were regarded with contempt.

The TUC was also treated with contempt by union members who asked for backing during disputes and failed to get it. Its leadership has a long history of taking the easy way out. They would describe it as the reasonable and pragmatic way.

Today it is run with a professionalism that its predecessors, stuck in a nostalgic rut and unable or unwilling to climb into the modern age, would not recognise. The annual TUC conference has only a third of the delegates that took part when it was at its peak but has become businesslike and focused.

Some might yearn for the bad old days – they were so exciting, after all – but today's TUC reflects the new trade unionism, which is what its members need.

# Sisters aren't doing it

There has never been a female general secretary of the TUC and only a handful of women union leaders. Which shows what a male-dominated world the unions live in.

Yet today more trade unionists are women (52 per cent) than men. Amazing when you consider that the only woman Prime Minister the UK has had was the sworn enemy of trade unions.

It is now the norm for women to work and despite huge leaps in 'family friendly' employment policies and a greater awareness of the importance of a work–life balance, the responsibility for child and home care still largely rests with the mother. Indeed, there is growing evidence to suggest that many women would prefer to raise their children than juggle the demands of work and home. Maybe the much-derided Wages for Housework campaign from the 1970s may yet see a resurgence.

There are good reasons for questioning the point of a woman slogging away at work all day, then getting home to slog away over the stove and ironing board, putting the children to bed, getting the children up and dashing off for another day on the treadmill. It is different for women far up the work scale. They have nannies and other kinds of help. The Supermum who can cope with six children and a job that brings in a million a year should try coping with two kids on an estate in Gateshead and a job in the fish-finger factory.

Yet there is growing pressure on mothers to get back to work almost as soon as their baby's umbilical cord is cut and send the brood off to a nursery for forty hours a week, even though there are concerns about the effect on children spending their early years like that.

Women still get paid far less than men and are poorly represented in many trades and professions. Which makes you wonder whether unions have fought as hard for sisters as they have for brothers.

As everyone knows from grainy images of the Second World War showing cheerful dungaree-clad gals in munitions factories or threshing hay, millions of women went to work, taking over 'men's jobs'. As soon as the war was over and returning servicemen needed employment, women were packed off back to the kitchen. But Pandora's box had been opened and ever since then many men (and some unsisterly women) have been trying to push the lid firmly back down on women at work.

Men are ten times more likely than women to be employed in skilled trades (19 per cent compared with 2 per cent) and are also more likely to be managers and senior officials. A fifth of women in employment do administrative or secretarial work compared with just 4 per cent of men.

There are 152,000 male cleaners working in the UK and 454,000 women; 465,000 male engineers and only 35,000 women – less than 10 per cent.

If there was equal representation across jobs there wouldn't be any excuse for some newspapers to gratuitously print photographs of pretty girls in the armed services, flying planes, driving trains, working on construction sites or in laboratories. It's the Barbie-in-uniform fantasy of many a (male) picture editor along with the flimsy-frocked fillies celebrating their A-level results in late summer, usually leaping in the air. Don't any boys pass exams? And how would the same papers fill their comment pages without sneering attacks on the appearance and, by inference, the abilities of female politicians (Blair's Babes, Cameron's Cuties) and businesswomen if there were as many women as men in those roles? (Since you ask, there are 143 women out of 650 MPs and only 10 per cent of the directors of the UK's top 100 companies are female.)

There are more women than men in health, public services, administration and personnel and customer services. By 2013 there will be more women GPs than men yet there is a chronic shortage of male primary school teachers (a notoriously poorly paid branch of teaching). The

Equal Pay Act became law in 1970 but obviously news has been slow to reach certain parts of the country. In 2010 an employment tribunal found in favour of women working for Birmingham City Council who were excluded from bonuses paid to their male colleagues, which meant the men were taking home four times as much as the women. Incidentally, this followed a remorseless battle by their union, sometimes in the face of male hostility.

There is still a pay gap of around 17 per cent between men and women and while some of that is due to more women than men taking a career break, working part time and generally putting family before work, it's also about a skills gap which stems from school, careers advice, access to education and training and perception.

Which brings us to the marvellous world of clichés and stereotypes favoured by the media when it comes to women at work. On the screen women at the top of their professions are either hard-bitten, lonely creatures who've sacrificed personal relationships for the job – think of the wonderful Helen Mirren in *Prime Suspect*, Hermione Norris in *Spooks* or Meryl Streep in *The Devil Wears Prada* – or plucky troupers holding families and communities together in soaps and sitcoms from Albert Square to Borchester.

While the trade union movement has an admirable record in promoting training and education, it has a pretty abysmal record in promoting women within its own ranks. The male-dominated unions traditionally fought to safeguard male-dominated employment in manufacturing and industry, with scant regard for women who could have stepped into a changing workplace had that not been viewed as a change too far.

Although women make up 52 per cent of union membership, that figure is unevenly distributed among the unions. In the manufacturing, technical, skilled and professional union of Amicus, now part of Unite, women form 27 per cent of the membership while among the mainly white- and blue-collar members of the former Transport and General Workers' Union they number only 22 per cent. Yet women make up 77 per cent of Unison, the public sector union, 58 per cent of the shop workers' and retail union USDAW and 60 per cent of the civil service union PCS. You won't be surprised to hear that while 78 per cent of the membership of the National Union of Teachers are women, they comprise just 2 per cent of the construction trades union UCATT.

There has been some progress in the representation of women in trade unions as branch organisers and officers, partly due to the growing proportion of women members. It is true that the annual gathering of the TUC is less over-bearingly masculine than it used to be. But if the trade union movement is to survive and remain relevant to working people, it needs to actively remove the barriers women face in getting union leadership roles, which are very similar to those they encounter in the workplace generally. There must also be recognition of the experience, skills and needs that women bring to the union power base beyond simply gender representation. As for black and minority ethnic women, who are the group most likely to belong to a union, they are severely under-represented.

Women are incredibly good at organising themselves and managing different tasks at the same time (men can do that too, of course – some can watch television *and* drink lager simultaneously). So they can cope with the demands of union work in addition to their other roles.

They won't be walked all over, either, or patronised. Remember the excruciating slow handclap given to Tony Blair by the Women's Institute? If the WI can do it to the Prime Minister, union women can do it to their bosses.

Politicians have belatedly recognised the importance of the women's vote – look how they were falling over themselves to get on Mumsnet.com during the election. It really is beyond the time when the unions should catch up.

# Baroness Dean of Thornton-le-Fylde aka Brenda

Anyone who thinks Margaret Thatcher was the greatest role model for a political woman should look at Brenda Dean.

Born in Salford, she left school at sixteen and soon became involved in the union movement. Not an easy life choice for a young woman in those days and she made it even harder for herself because the union was SOGAT, the printers' union, which believed women could be employed as long as they stuck to making tea and typing the occasional letter. Yet she went on to become its general secretary, the first female head of any British trade union, entering the House of Lords when SOGAT merged with Amicus.

Mrs Thatcher is remembered for fighting the unions. Brenda Dean fought the male-dominated hierarchy in SOGAT, the anarchic industrial relations of Fleet Street, the toughest employers (R. Murdoch, Esq.) and the swiftest, most all-encompassing change in working practices after the Wapping dispute.

Now there's a real female role model.

# Billy and Arthur

Millions have seen a version of it by watching *Billy Elliot* but there is still nothing that can completely capture the drama, the bitterness, the anger and frustration of the miners' strike of 1984–5. There has never been anything like it in modern times – maybe ever in this country – and there certainly never will be again.

The miners were the shock troops of the trade union movement. They were tough, they were united, they were determined. Always had been. It had been a miners' dispute which led to the General Strike in 1926. The miners who beat Edward Heath in 1974. Their industry was in decline but there were still 187,000 employed in it.

In 1981, two years after Mrs Thatcher came to power, the miners fought for a pay rise and won again. That was the turning point. She was determined not just to never be beaten by them again but to smash them and, by crushing the miners, to wreck the union movement.

Several things happened after 1981. Mrs Thatcher put a brutal American industrialist of Scottish extraction called Ian MacGregor in charge of the National Coal Board and began stockpiling huge quantities of coal. The laws against unions had been toughened but she also created a police force that was equipped with riot shields and batons. They looked as if they were going to war, and they were. Against the miners.

The other major change was the retirement of the leadership of the National Union of Mineworkers and the elevation of Arthur Scargill, firebrand boss of the Yorkshire regional NUM, to general secretary. Scargill was not just highly political but dogmatic, stubborn, blinkered and unbending. Thatcher–MacGregor–Scargill – it was a threesome made in hell.

The spark that lit the blue touch paper was the provocative proposal by MacGregor to close twenty pits with the loss of 20,000 jobs. Scargill the pugilist balloted his members to ask if they would strike if this plan went ahead. They said 'Yes', since no one really believed it would. Scargill never again held a ballot, using the result he'd got to launch all-out war.

That led to immediate divisions in the union. Pit supervisors, who were members of a different union, NACODS, refused to come out. They argued that without maintenance the pits would deteriorate and be closed anyway, which would defeat the point of the strike.

But most damaging was the refusal of the miners in Nottinghamshire to join the strike. So not only were there large stacks of coal that would last for months but more was still being mined in many of the most productive pits in the country.

# The Falklands, part two

Mrs Thatcher had beaten the Argentinians in the Falklands and now she was determined to secure victory over what she called 'the enemy within', a despicable way to describe working men whose fathers and grandfathers had fought and died for their country in two world wars.

She set her army of police on the pickets. Brutal battles

ensued day after day as lorries drove out with coal and, later, when desperate strikers were forced back to work (remember *Billy Elliot*?), as coaches carried them into the pits. Mounted police charged picket lines, making an encounter between Millwall and West Ham supporters look like the Chelsea Flower Show.

Yet the bitterness was not only against the government and the Coal Board but within the mining communities, particularly when it looked as if police brutality was being used to protect blacklegs and scabs.

Travel restrictions were brought in to stop striking miners crossing county boundaries to support other pickets. That didn't apply to the police: they had astonishing powers which were regarded as an outright attack on democracy and the right to strike. Other forces supplied reinforcements in their thousands because it was feared local officers would be 'too sympathetic' to the strikers.

The government even seemed prepared to starve the striking miners back to work by banning their families from claiming welfare benefits. With no wages and no other means of support other than charity and strike funds, extreme poverty ravaged the mining communities. People were up to their eyes in debt. Is it any wonder that gradually more and more miners had to take the difficult decision to return to work?

By the beginning of 1985, defeat was staring the miners

# THE POP QUIZ!

The miners' strike inspired many artists to write and record songs in support of this epic industrial dispute. Can you match the performers with the songs? Answers on page 177.

| | |
|---|---|
| **Manic Street Preachers** | 1985 |
| **Pulp** | Iron Hand |
| **Ewan MacColl** | Last Day of the Miners' Strike |
| **Sting** | Stone's Throw Away |
| **Billy Bragg** | We Work the Black Seam |
| **U2** | Which Side Are You On? |
| **Chumbawamba** | Fitzwilliam |
| **Dire Straits** | Daddy, What Did You Do in the Strike? |
| **Paul Weller** | Red Hill Mining Town |

in the face. Everyone knew it. Everyone, that is, but Arthur Scargill. He fought on until even he had to accept defeat, one year to the day after the strike began.

Scargill had warned at the beginning that the plan was not to axe twenty pits but to reduce the 170 then operating to below a hundred. No one believed him. This is an island built on coal and it was ridiculous to think the number of mines could be that low. But today there are four pits in Britain. Even Arthur Scargill couldn't have imagined this once magnificent, proud industry would be so utterly destroyed, leaving terrible social scars in former mining areas where there is little or no work.

However smug Thatcher and MacGregor might have been, there were no real winners of this terrible dispute. Except for the women, who fought their own glorious battle. The miners' WAGS were the real heroes, organising communal kitchens, collections and benefit concerts. For many women in traditional mining communities, this was a bitterly hard introduction to politics and feminist radicalism. But how they rose to the challenge.

# Don't pick that scab!

The most derisory, insulting, virulent, word in the trade union lexicon is 'scab'. It is not spoken, it is spat out. A scab is the worst form of human life – sub-human, really. Worse, even, than a Tory.

Middle-class children grow up thinking that scabs are things that sprout on your knee after you have fallen over. You pick them and they bleed. Working-class children grew up knowing that scabs are traitors and outcasts who are picked by the bosses to break strikes, and make your heart bleed when your strike then collapses.

Politicians of all breeds have talked a lot about 'community' in the past few years. They say that many of the woes in the country today are due to the loss of a sense of community, such as there was in the good old days.

As it happens, there was never much of a feeling of community among the middle classes. They kept themselves to themselves on the whole. It was in the working-class areas where it existed, often fostered by a high proportion of the residents working in the same industry, even for the same company.

Solidarity wasn't just a platitude from a book by a Marxist academic. It was how these people lived their lives. And never did it matter more than in difficult times, particularly when there was a strike or threatened redundancies (or lay-offs, as they used to be called).

The person who continued to work when the rest of their mates were on strike and who crossed the picket line was a scab. Like Billy Elliot's dad.

The most minor punishment that was inflicted on a scab was to send him to Coventry. (If you think this isn't much of a punishment, have you ever spent a wet Sunday afternoon there?) It really isn't pleasant to be shunned, ignored and not spoken to. It is rather like eating with teenagers.

# Requiem for the picket line

Strikes and pickets go together like fish and chips. There

are very different kinds of picketing, although all have the same aim – to deter others from working and stop anything productive happening in the place being picketed.

Picketing used to vary from a small number of people standing outside the place of work and handing out leaflets to workmates who were still going in, to massive demonstrations of hundreds, even thousands, battling to stop blacklegs breaking the strike and lorries continuing to get in and out of the plant.

Needless to say, mass picketing has been banned (yes, Mrs Thatcher yet again). But, for old times' sake, let's take a walk down memory lane and look at the various kinds of pickets there used to be:

★ **Informational picketing.** Fundamentally doing what it says on the label. Standing there and letting people know what is going on. Still allowed.

★ **Basic picketing.** A slightly more robust version. You ask people not to cross your picket line. There is usually a certain amount of banter. Bosses walk by with their eyes cast downward. Disloyal colleagues stare brazenly ahead, their gaze wavering neither to right nor left (though their political views have surely wavered far to the right). Pickets will call out occasional abusive comments. Some non-strikers will stop to talk; perhaps to explain their position and then carry on into work, while a few may actually be persuaded and refuse to cross the picket line. They may even join the line! Still allowed but with a maximum of six pickets.

★ **Mass pickets.** Everyone, but everyone, turned out. Not just the people directly involved in the dispute but their friends, neighbours, fellow trade unionists, blokes who wanted to show a bit of solidarity, lads who fancied a barney, left-wing agitators. . . the lot. They would block roads and obstruct entrances. They would shout a lot, particularly when a lorry or coach was trying to get in.

★ Flying pickets. The SAS of industrial action. They would swoop to wherever they were most needed, arriving suddenly when pickets were feeling overwhelmed or outnumbered by police to add their weight to the battle.

★ Secondary picketing. Picketing somewhere which is not directly concerned in the dispute (a lorry depot, for example) or where people not directly involved in a strike join picketers who are. (Covered more fully in 'Coming second' on pages 87–8.)

Governments have done their damnedest down the years to neuter the effects of picketing. After the General Strike in 1926, mass picketing was made illegal, although that didn't stop mass pickets continuing to take place from time to time.

The sop offered to unions to try to persuade them that the anti-picketing laws are not all one-sided is that the law gives protection to pickets 'who are acting in connection with an industrial dispute at or near their workplace and are using their picketing to peacefully obtain or communicate information or peacefully persuade any person to work or abstain from working'. This legalistic gobbledegook means that if pickets are good little people and don't upset anyone, employers (or anyone else) can't sue them. This hasn't stopped companies applying for and getting injunctions to curb the effects of picketing (i.e. make them pointless).

As ever, the bosses find a way round the law while the judges make sure workers and unions can't.

## Pickets, my arse

The image which Ricky Tomlinson projects when he appears on TV is of an affable, if grumpy, old git. That isn't how he was portrayed thirty-eight years ago.

In those days he was a union activist in the building trade, which was bedevilled with a system called 'the lump'. It had been devised by employers to avoid the rights the union had won for its members and involved hiring men who weren't in the union, paying them cash in hand and forgetting about any safety rules or agreements on hours and conditions.

The builders' union called a strike on selected sites in 1972, the main aim being to get rid of the lump. Although many members answered the call and came out, there was a problem in the Shrewsbury area, where some sites went on working.

So a big picket was organised for the town, with many men coming from far afield. It passed off peacefully, though. There were no arrests and the police chief in charge of controlling the picket congratulated them on their conduct.

Two months later, however, the Home Secretary ordered a high-level police inquiry into 'violent picketing' at Shrewsbury. This followed building industry bosses handing him a dossier which consisted almost exclusively of press cuttings (and you can imagine what they said).

A number of activists, including Ricky Tomlinson, were arrested and charged with offences including affray, unlawful assembly and conspiracy, based on an Act of Parliament of 1875. The lawyers must have spent a long time tracking that one down.

At the trial, the prosecuting counsel set the tone by describing the picket as 'like a swarm of Apache Indians',

Having a reputation as a union militant makes it hard to find a job. Ricky Tomlinson had to model string vests but his new career took off when he moved on to (almost) complete vests.

Mirrorpix

clearly a terrifying prospect for any juror who had watched a B-movie Western about the Indian uprising in Shropshire.

The prosecution didn't rely on cuttings from the *Daily Express*. It produced a witness who said he had heard the pickets shouting 'Kill! Kill! Kill!' This was true. Those words had been uttered. But they weren't shouting 'Kill the cops/fuzz/pigs' but 'Kill, kill the lump!' The fact that no police officer – or picket – was injured and no arrests were made on the day might indicate that not a lot of violence, let alone attempted murder, took place. It was clearly a complete load of scaremongering bollocks. Not to a British jury it wasn't.

Three of the Shrewsbury pickets were sent to jail and two of them, Ricky Tomlinson and Des Warren, were kept inside for three years despite a series of walk-outs on building sites and the docks in their support, a march from Wigan to London demanding a general strike and pressure on the TUC and the Labour Party after it came to power in 1974. The union leadership abandoned them but trade unionists throughout the country showed fantastic solidarity.

After being found guilty, Ricky said from the dock: 'Politically motivated interference by governments acting on behalf of and under political pressure from employers now means that no trade unionist can enter freely into negotiations with employers. They cannot withdraw their labour – the only thing they possess as a bargaining lever – without being accused of setting out to wreck the economy, of challenging the law. The building employers, by their contempt of the laws governing safety regulations, are guilty of causing the deaths and maiming of workers – yet they are not dealt with by the courts.'

So next time you see him grumbling away on the *Royle Family* sofa, remember that what he really wants to say is: 'British justice? My arse!!!'

# Coming second

Going on strike is a serious business and no one should enter into industrial action without being determined to win. By whatever means, within reason.

One good device invented early on was secondary picketing. This is how it worked. Say there was a strike at a factory employing 200 people. The company had two other factories, each employing another 200. So these 400 came along to the factory where the action was and joined the picket line. Then the people who drove the lorries that usually carried the goods joined in, too, even though they worked for another company altogether.

Secondary picketing focused the minds of employers not only because a dispute would escalate quickly but because other employers would begin to be affected and start pressing to get things sorted out. Good, eh?

Unfortunately, when Mrs Thatcher was Prime Minister she gave legal power to the hackneyed phrase 'all good things must come to an end'. She ended all sorts of practices the trade unions had been up to and chief among these was secondary picketing.

Now it is no longer lawful to picket outside somewhere which is not your direct and usual place of business. Even if the workers hold a ballot and say they want to join in.

The reason given was that the balance of power during

industrial disputes had swung towards the unions. This was true, but from a point which was so much in the employers' favour, unions had little power to start with. If it had swung any further towards the employers, it would have been like living in serfdom again.

But as the unions worked out new tactics, fought for more powers and organised more effectively, so the Thatcher government redressed the balance (Harold Wilson's Labour government had tried to do something similar, though not as bad, a decade earlier, but chickened out in the face of stiff union opposition).

The crushing of secondary picketing wasn't as violent as some of the things the Tories did but it made peaceful picketing a lot less effective. And not effective at all if some workers are prepared to cross picket lines.

## Socialist Workers plc

The Socialist Workers Party is the entrepreneur of left-wing ideology. It never misses an opportunity to exploit a dispute, demonstration, picket, rally or any other public gathering where its all-purpose banners and placards can be brandished.

Considering it is a tiny sect, it has remarkable tentacles and sources of information. How do they discover the least significant of events and manage to turn up with appropriate signs held aloft?

Some carry all-purpose slogans, such as 'FIGHT THE CUTS', 'STOP THE WAR', 'SUPPORT THE BOYCOTT' and the long-time favourite, now sadly redundant, 'BLAIR MUST GO'.

But, like all good entrepreneurs, they are quick to refine the product for the situation, so pickets and demonstrators have got used to seeing appropriate slogans on the placards handed out to them, for example: 'BACK THE DORKING THREE', 'JUSTICE FOR BRIAN JELLY' or 'NO CUTS AT SHORE FOUNDRY' and countless variations that have miraculously appeared down the years.

What they all have in common is the logo blazoned across the top: 'Socialist Worker'. No capitalist organisation was ever as efficient at creating publicity for itself, especially as the only cost is a bit of paper, a wooden stick and some printing ink. No multi-million advertising bills for the SWP, comrades.

How do they get away with it? Why has no strike committee ever said to them 'Sorry, mates, take your posters elsewhere'? The answer must surely be that when a strike/ picket/demonstration is organised and someone asks 'Shouldn't we get some placards printed?' the easy reply is 'No point. The SWP is bound to be along with theirs.'

To the politically ignorant, it looks as if every march,

dispute etc. has been organised by the SWP. This is presumably what they want the world to think. But their involvement doesn't bring the revolution a nanosecond nearer. In fact, it is unlikely that the vast majority of people involved in an industrial dispute, including those carrying SWP posters, have a clue what their politics is. Some form of socialism, sure. But what exactly? Don't know, don't care. Can you carry this now, my arm's aching.

# And now for something a bit different

Workers don't have to go on strike to take industrial action (incidentally, action is called industrial even if it has nothing to do with industry). There are all sorts of other ways they can withdraw their labour, some more subtle than others.

A favourite used to be the **go-slow**. As its name so clearly implies, this consisted of workers, er. . . going slow. This might have been easy to do if the people involved were working on a production line and they turned its speed down so that it churned through only five cars an hour instead of eight. But how do you go slow if you are a teacher? Or a probation worker? Or a journalist? Do you not shout at pupils as often, reform fewer criminals or write less scurrilous stories?

Then there was the **work to rule**. This was based on the principle that workers were doing far more than they were contracted to do. Not a concept that was borne out by many people who worked in British industry in the 1970s. So it came down to being bloody awkward. 'Could you bring me in that folder on the Roberts case, please?' 'Sorry, Mr Andrews, that's Janine's job and she's not in today.'

The big problem with much of British industry used to be that workers insisted on working to rule all the time – at least, what they considered to be the very strict rules that made life easier for them. Nowadays they work a lot harder, are far more flexible, give bosses all sorts of things they strictly speaking don't need to and would never dream of 'working to rule'. In other words: Bosses 1; Workers 0.

**Banning overtime**. This is a baffling one. Employers pay overtime not because they are generous but because it saves them having to hire more people. Workers like it as it boosts their inadequate wages. Refusing to do it may hurt the company a bit but it hurts the workers a lot more, especially if they rely on it to get their income beyond subsistence level. So banning overtime hurts the workers more than the bosses. You might as well go the whole hog and go on strike.

**The mandatory meeting**. This was a rather cunning

ruse developed in the newspaper industry. What happened was that the workers (if we can be forgiven for referring to them as such) would call a union meeting in a crucial production period, which everyone had to attend. Mandatory, you see. So, as a result, no work was done while they listened to long speeches and decided whether or not they would take action (as if they weren't by holding the meeting). There was a ritual to these activities (as there is to much of union business). The officials would gather in the meeting place and the members would gradually drift in. Someone would be sent to make sure no one was still at their work station. This would take up a few more minutes. After about an hour, a letter was received from management saying: 'Your meeting is now interfering with production.' Forty-five minutes later, another missive would arrive: 'Your meeting is now seriously interfering with production. Would you please return to work?' When the third begging letter arrived, it would be put to the vote: 'That this meeting be adjourned'. There was then a debate on this, during which a fourth letter arrived, this time a mixture of hysteria and whiny pleading. It could, of course, be ignored as the matter was already the subject of debate. When the vote was finally taken, the members would agree to adjourn until the next day (same time, same place) if they wanted to keep up the pressure or next week, if they thought the management might now have got the message that it needed to up the offer. If the dispute was already deadlocked, they might vote not to return to work so the meeting went on. And possibly on. What difference there was between this and a strike was a fine point only appreciated by the officials. Who were also the only people capable of speaking for ten hours about such trivialities as the size of a weekly allowance.

**Non-co-operation**. Another good one, this, and quite baffling to anyone not up to speed on the complexities of industrial life. To the initiated, it would appear to be a version of the work to rule. But there is a subtle difference. Whereas that is more formal – 'these are rules, we are sticking doggedly to them' – non-co-operation is simply. . . well, not co-operating. So it's a lot more flexible. So flexible, in fact, that anything goes. How about not co-operating by failing to turn up for work? Or going to a different plant? Or coming in at wildly wrong times? Or refusing to do a particular piece of work? Alternatively, it could be something quite minor, like not co-operating by not flushing the lavatory after use (though this is not minor for the eighth person to use it). Or refusing to put stamps on envelopes before posting them.

What these different forms of industrial action have in common is that they are designed to cause maximum annoyance and disruption to the bosses with minimum inconvenience and loss of income to the workers. Sadly, they have not just gone out of fashion but been rendered pretty pointless by the anti-union laws. Any industrial action must be balloted on and if you are going to ballot on a go-slow or work to rule, you might as well go the whole hog and ballot on a strike.

How sad that this industrial guerrilla warfare has passed into history with the cannon and the bayonet.

# The General Strike

There have been two world wars but only one general strike, at least in this country. It is very much *the* General Strike and is still talked of with reverence in the Labour movement, even though it is unlikely that more than a few people who took part in it are still alive.

On 3 May 1926, the miners walked out (sound familiar?) in an attempt to prevent a reduction in their wages. This was an entirely justifiable dispute, particularly as the miners were doing their dirty, dangerous job for a pittance while the mine owners were fat, rich bastards who wanted to squeeze miners' pay so they could buy more Cuban cigars and French champagne. (If coal went up in price, that wouldn't have worried them – they could just have put another servant on the fire.)

In a unique act of solidarity, the general council of the TUC declared a general strike, giving notice that other workers would come out in support of the miners.

Even without a general strike, this was serious. In those days there were a million miners. So the Tory government attempted to broker a deal. Before that could be done, though, the blue touch paper for confrontation was lit when the printers at the *Daily Mail* refused to print an editorial headed 'For King and Country'. Now there are many things working people can do and the government will turn a discreet blind eye, but refusing to print an editorial in the *Daily Mail*, especially one so patriotic and anti-worker, was too much.

The General Strike was on. Millions of workers throughout the country came out, even though the Labour Party, still reeling from the forged Zinoviev letter 'revealing' a Communist plot, which had appeared in (yes, you've guessed it) the *Daily Mail* a couple of years earlier, was quaking in its boots about what they saw as subversive revolutionary elements in the unions (nothing changes, does it?). Not only did the pits stop but buses, trains, lorries, the docks and a lot more.

The government reacted by mobilising a special militia of God-fearing and union-hating middle-class folk who did things like drive buses and lorries. They had always wanted to do that (it was so much more fun than those dull pen-pushing jobs they normally did) and being able to rub the noses of the strikers in the dirt at the same time made it a double whammy. Huge stockpiles of coal had been put by and police baton-charged pickets, two tactics which Mrs Thatcher used sixty years later. The Catholic Church came out on the side of the bosses, condemning the strike as a sin. A government propaganda sheet, the *British Gazette*, was produced under the editorship of Winston Churchill (something working people never forgave him for, even after World War Two).

After ten days, in a move which to this day is seen as arrant cowardice, the TUC called off the strike. It stuttered on momentarily but it was all over.

Never again has there been a general strike in this country. It is as if that defeat so scarred the Labour movement that it couldn't bring itself to once more embark on such all-encompassing action.

# When in Rome

Contrary to popular belief, the 1926 stoppage was not unique in the history of the world, however much very old trade unionists look back wistfully on it.

The first general strike was the *secessio plebis* in Rome in 494BC. The plebeians – or plebs as they were known for short and, subsequently, for abuse – were the Roman citi-

The first general strike took place in Rome in 494BC. The vote was: in favour of strike – 1; against strike – 2,386. But the one in favour had the sword, so the vote was carried.

zens who did all the work. The posh people relied on them for everything. They probably couldn't even brush their teeth on their own, any more than Prince Charles can.

When the plebs wanted something or got fed up at the behaviour of their masters, they got this great idea of simply walking out. Out of their shops and workshops, out of Rome, up into the surrounding hills. You can imagine what happened then. All those Romans in their togas running around shouting, gripping the laurel wreaths on their heads, their wives screaming at them to get the plebs back because there weren't any candles to light the dinner table – or for that matter anything to put on the dinner table. The children (little brats) hysterical because their favourite toy couldn't be repaired as the workshop round the corner was closed.

It wouldn't have taken long for some of the upper orders to go crawling up into the hills and beg them to return. Now that's a good way for a strike to end.

The masters didn't learn their lesson, though. There were four more *secessiones plebis* before they finally accepted that even plebs have rights, the fifth and final *secessio* wringing from them the *Lex Hortensia*, the law which ended the class struggle between patricians and plebeians.

Unfortunately, eighty-five years after our general strike, the struggle between British patricians and plebeians continues.

# Political strikes

Political strikes have never really caught on in this country. British workers have just not been interested in withdrawing their labour to achieve a political end.

That isn't how the *Daily Mail* sees it. In common with other right-wing newspapers and politicians, they spy a dangerous plot lurking in just about every workplace. Whenever industrial action is threatened, let alone taken, it is portrayed as part of a lethal plan to bring about the collapse of civilisation as we know it.

Now it is true that there are some trade unionists who would like to foment revolution and use 'the workers' to man the barricades. But they are a very small number. Very, very small. At least, they used to be very, very small. Nowadays they are very, very, very, very, very small.

There has occasionally been a time when a politically motivated official (a phrase used by the Labour Prime Minister Harold Wilson to describe the leaders of industrial action by seamen in the 1960s – one of whom was John Prescott, who went on to become deputy Prime Minister in the 1990s and has just taken his seat in the House of Lords) might use a normal industrial demand as the front for a bigger battle. Perhaps he would fantasise that a strike for a modest pay rise would have incredible knock-on effects (government falls, Prime Minister flees country, royal family sent to live in dog kennel on the Isle of Wight). But the workers have never been that easily fooled. They could always see the difference between wanting an extra couple of quid a week and dreaming of a socialist republic.

It did happen in Russia, but that was almost a century ago and now that country's capitalism makes the USA's look pink. And while there have been revolutions in other countries, the army tended to be involved. So it wasn't so much a socialist revolution as a military coup. Not quite what Joe the wild-eyed shop steward wanted.

Just about every big dispute in Britain, from the General Strike on, has been carried out against a background of accusations that it is political. The miners' strike was political, said Mrs Thatcher. Well, yes, it was – she made it so by using new laws and battalions of riot police to beat the shit out of the miners.

You always had to be quite eccentric (to put it politely) to think you could foment a political strike in this country. Today, in an era in which workers are more worried about their mortgages, the special offers at Tesco and who lost the remote control down the back of the settee, only an utterly barking mad, 24-carat nutter would think revolution was in the air. If anyone has seen one of those individuals in the past decade, would they kindly put a stamp on him and post him to the left wing of the Priory.

Union hardliners even manage to do more for the Tories and their friends in the boss class than for the working class. It wasn't only Mrs Thatcher who used accusations of political strikes being fomented to bring in the police – or even the army, as Winston Churchill as Home Secretary did before the First World War – or introduce anti-union legislation. The Winter of Discontent wasn't a political strike but it had enormous political consequences, leading to the election of the Thatcher government and all that meant.

The creation of the Labour Party by the union movement was supposed to provide a vehicle for representing the working class politically, thus making it unnecessary to use more robust means to achieve change. Ha ha ha. The Labour Party was soon infiltrated by people dedicated to subverting it to such dangerous dogmas as unfettered capitalism and militarism.

At its annual conference, the TUC's delegates continue to pass political motions as if they had political Delhi belly. Motions on what the government should be doing and not doing, what other countries should be doing, boycotting this and uniting with that. But the only action involved is putting up their hands when it's time to vote.

In his heart, even the most wild-eyed union boss knows that the theme song of the British revolutionary is 'You'll Always Walk Alone.' Sad, isn't it?

## Now is the winter of our discontent...

1978. The year of *Dallas*, *The Deer Hunter* and Kevin Keegan's perm. It was also the year that marked the beginning of the end of the mighty unions.

Three years before, with inflation at an unbelievable 26.9 per cent, Harold Wilson's Labour government had reached a deal with the TUC limiting pay rises to £6 a week for anyone earning less than £8,500 a year . By 1978, inflation had more than halved but the government, now led by Jim Callaghan, still wanted a 5 per cent cap on pay increases.

The unions were furious. They wanted a return to free collective bargaining so they could negotiate their own deals on behalf of their members. The Ford Motor Company set a pay rise within the 5 per cent limit but it was rejected by its employees, 15,000 of whom walked out. Within days, a further 57,000 had joined them and twenty-three Ford plants across the UK lay idle. The Transport and General Workers' Union (TGWU) hit Ford with a 25 per cent pay demand for a 35-hour week and after protracted negotiations agreed a 17 per cent rise. The strikers went back to work and peace descended. But that wasn't the end of it. The government was livid that Ford had broken its pay policy, for that made it powerless to impose a 5 per cent limit on anyone else. And so it proved.

The car workers were followed by lorry drivers, who were after a 40 per cent rise. Petrol stations closed, striking drivers picketed ports and refineries, and anything that should have been delivered by road wasn't. After a month on strike, the lorry drivers got a pay deal of just £1 less than they'd wanted. At the same time, public sector workers walked out, demanding wage increases in line with those the private sector had agreed.

On 22 January 1979, there was a 'Day of Action' in which 1.5 million workers walked out. It was the biggest stoppage of work in the UK since the General Strike more than half a century earlier. Mass demonstrations were held across the country. Schools and airports were closed, ambulance drivers struck, as did nurses, although 999 calls and emergencies were dealt with. Many strikers didn't go back but stayed out. These included gravediggers and dustmen. Piles of rat-infested rubbish in London's Leicester Square became a powerful image of a weak government and a country held to ransom by the unions.

By the end of February, most strikers had returned to work but the UK had lost a total of 29,474,000 working days to strike action. It had been anarchy, with the unions losing control of their members and Jim Callaghan's Labour government losing control of everything.

So who was the victor of the Winter of Discontent? That's easy. Not the workers who got huge pay rises but a certain Mrs Margaret Thatcher. On the back of public disquiet at what appeared to be happening to the country, she swept to power at the election in May. The rest, as they say, is history.

# The reverse strike: a cunning trick

A lock-out is the opposite of a strike. It is a strike by bosses against their workers. The employees want to work but they can't.

This usually happens when the union is taking some form of industrial action short of a strike or maybe is planning or threatening a strike. Let's say that a work to rule is being held. The bosses are getting exasperated. They say they can't operate the factory properly under these conditions. The union says: 'Tough – meet our demands.'

At that stage the company says: 'OK, if you won't work as you are supposed to, you won't work at all.' The gates are locked and when people turn up they are sent away. They can see the bosses glowering out at them from behind a window. Probably puffing away at a fat cigar, in the days when smoking was allowed at work and bosses were allowed to glower.

The idea was that the workers would be so upset at being locked out, they would capitulate and the factory would then be reopened.

An even more petulant use of the lock-out was when the union announced it was planning a strike or thinking of striking. If that's your attitude, the antediluvian employers would snarl, tweaking their moustaches and gobbing into a spittoon, you can do it now. And they would stop them coming to work in a pre-emptive strike. You knew these bosses were dying to say 'Now see how you like it!'

The lock-out appears to have fallen into disuse in recent years. Perhaps employers have become slightly more enlightened. Or perhaps the legal insistence on strike ballots creates some sort of problem for employers.

Who knows? Who cares? The lock-out was a nasty tool in the industrial war and it never had a place in good relations at work.

## Zzzzzzzzzzzzzzzzzzzzzzz. . .

It is inescapably true that people interested in attending dull, interminable meetings and immersing themselves in the intricacies of procedure gravitate to becoming trade union officials.

The sort of geeks who would have become lawyers if they had been born into middle-class homes tend to fasten on their union as a way of spending many an excruciating hour absorbed in the minutiae of The Rule Book, which is a cross between the Highway Code and the Lisbon Treaty.

If David Attenborough ever did a programme on the habitat of the union activist, he would film a strange, shabby place indeed. A few old chairs of extraordinary uncomfortableness set out in rows in front of a battered and stained table behind which the chairman and secretary sit.

Here is one description of a union meeting: 'It is something like torture to sit through the long, repetitive, self-important ramblings of committee members who turn up for meetings and do little else.' That wasn't written by some bored dullard who couldn't be bothered playing his part but by an official of the University and College Union – which you might think was one of those with the more exciting agendas.

The fact is, though, that if there weren't people prepared to go through that boring stuff, there wouldn't be unions and there wouldn't be organisations ready to take up the fight when the fight needs to be taken up.

Ignoring meetings and sneering at the faithful few who can be bothered to play an active role is rather like refusing to attend football training sessions because they are boring and repetitive, and it is only the games which are exciting.

That is not to say that this is a book which is going to urge you to turn up on the first Tuesday in the month to attend every branch meeting. If you're not that way inclined, don't bother making the effort, as the actress said to the bishop.

But that doesn't mean you shouldn't at least keep an eye on what is going on from time to time. Just so you know what is being done in your name. And even turning up occasionally, to show you care.

Assuming that there may be at least a few people reading this who are quite interested in participating, here are some basic facts about union meetings.

They are still to a great extent governed by what is

revered as the bible of running meetings, *The ABC of Chairmanship*, written in 1939 by Walter Citrine (then the general secretary of the TUC but later ennobled as Lord Citrine of Chairmanship in the County of Dank-CommitteeRoom). (Sad footnote: The treasured copy of *Citrine* owned by one of the authors of this book tragically disappeared during a bitter divorce.)

Calling it an ABC implies that this guide is making things easy (as in 'ABC, simple as one, two, three' – the Jackson Five). In fact, Citrine runs to 330 pages. By dotting every i and crossing every t, it can settle any argument (and there are certainly plenty of those to be dealt with) but it doesn't exactly make for simplicity.

Attendees at meetings can be divided into four types:

★ **The officials**. They are the ones in charge and want everyone else to know it. They may well have been doing the jobs for years and have no plans to stand down. It took them a long time to claw their way up to the exalted position of assistant branch secretary (Region Four) and they sure aren't going to give it up to some upstart whippersnapper.
★ **The upstart whippersnappers** who have only been in the union five minutes (or it may be five years, but time hangs heavy at union meetings) and want to take over the world.

★ **The old faithful**. They have been coming to meetings since time began and if they don't turn up for one, you know they have died. They rarely if ever say anything but can be relied upon to vote and always vote the way the branch officials want them to.

★ **The occasional attender.** This is someone who may have come in by accident or because someone said they should turn up and they stupidly have done or possibly they just felt it was right to put in an appearance because it was raining. They spend the meeting with a look of bemusement on their faces, as well they might in this surreal world. The look turns to one of terror when an official approaches them. It's probably only to say hello and welcome, but they are petrified that they will be asked to do something – take the minutes or sit on a sub-committee. The one basic rule for them is NEVER VOLUNTEER. Not for anything. Not even for putting out the chairs or stacking them afterwards. That way lies endless being volunteered for all sorts of tasks, just because you have shown willing.

# My Lords, Ladies and Comrades...

This is a true story. At a union meeting a few years ago, a heated debate was raging over whether a management pay offer should be accepted. The officials wanted it turned down but the members weren't convinced and it was beginning to look as if they would reject their officials' recommendation and say 'Yes', spoiling weeks of negotiation.

Then up stood one of the older members, a small Welshman known to all as 'Lippy'. Speaking slowly but with passion, in a few sentences he put forward an unanswerable case for why it was worth fighting for. The room fell silent. He paused for what seemed an age, then sat down.

Minutes later, the meeting voted and backed the officials. That one brief speech had turned the mood.

As the members filed out, one official said to another (OK, it was one of this book's authors): 'The great thing about Lippy isn't just that he knows what to say, he knows exactly when to stop.'

Later that day, it was discovered that the reason he had stopped when he did was that he felt a heart attack coming on. Fortunately he made a full recovery, though he never spoke at a union meeting again.

What happened to Lippy was a lesson about public speaking. Although fundamentally doing no more than talking to people you work with every day, it can be more stressful than having sex. Although, to our knowledge, no university has yet been given a grant to investigate the truth of that proposition.

It isn't essential to speak at union meetings. In fact, if everyone did every time, meetings would go on even longer than they do. And some people have an obsessive compulsion to get up and deliver an oration whenever they find themselves in a formal gathering of a few workmates.

The speakers at union meetings can be divided into four categories:

★ **Officials**. They have to speak but do they have to drone on and on and on and on and. . .? The best officials are concise and precise. They explain what they have to and leave it at that. They also understand that the members need to be allowed time to speak, too.

★ **Habitual speakers**. These can be split into three:
  • **Former officials** wanting to show off their knowledge and experience (they will start every intervention with 'When we were involved in the negotiations of 1983 – no, hold on, it was 1982'). And demonstrating they are not past it and really should still be in the positions they held with such distinction for over twenty years.
  • **The wannabes**. These are younger members who are pushing to take over from the current officials. They want to be noticed and use every opportunity to jump to their feet and put in their pennyworth.
  • **The verbal diahorreaists**. These aren't former offi-

cials, though they are convinced they should have been, or wannabes, though that may be because they have given up hope of advancement. But they have always spoken at union meetings and always will. When they get up to speak, a sigh runs round the room and some members get out that morning's crossword to pass the time.

★ **Occasional speakers**. They speak when they have something to say and when they know something about what is being discussed. The unsung heroes of union meetings.

★ **The silent majority**. They never speak. They sit mute while others orate around them. They may be described by cynical activists as the cannon fodder of the union movement but let's not be dismissive of them. At least they turn up to meetings.

# A load of old ballots

Their critics accuse the unions of being undemocratic but there can be few more democratic organisations since the Greek city states. They ballot on just about everything and the main complaint their leaders make is that not enough members take part.

It wasn't always like this, although voting has been at

Delegates respond to a request from the chairman: which is your right hand?

the core of unions since they began. Strike votes used to consist of hands up at a mass meeting. It was pretty intimidating for the seven members who didn't think they should take industrial action when they felt the eyes on them of the 6,326 comrades whose arms had shot up when asked 'All those in favour'. (Punctuation note: should there be a question mark at the end of those four words? Grammatically speaking, there should. But as anyone who has been at a union meeting will testify, 'All those in favour' isn't really uttered as a question, more an exhortation – sometimes even an instruction. No question mark there, then.)

Nowadays unions have to ballot on everything. For the election of all major officials. For procedural matters such as mergers and recognition. And, of course, for strikes and just about any other form of industrial action.

Ballots should, in theory, be a help to unions. They make it more complicated to set industrial action in motion (though there is no evidence that they have done anything to get strike proposals rejected, which is what Thatcher thought they'd do) but they give democratic legitimacy to whatever action is agreed.

That, at least, is the theory. It doesn't happen in real life, though – if you can call the right-wing press and the courts real life. To them, because they cannot understand, let alone accept, that anyone in their right mind would want to take action against their kind, benevolent employers, they look for any ludicrous excuse to invalidate the result of the ballot.

What they haven't worked out, because thinking logically doesn't come high on the list of 'must dos' for the right wing, is that workers feel more committed to an action if they have gone through a formal voting procedure.

The downside for unions is that ballots cost a lot of money to run. Which, of course, was part of the reason they were introduced. The Thatcher government's cunning plan was that unions would be less likely to want strikes if they had to find large sums to ballot members before calling them. They also patronisingly believed that union officials would think harder before plunging into industrial action if they had to go through the hassle, as well as finding the money, of organising a ballot. As if any strike was ever called because someone woke up one morning and thought 'What shall I do today? I know, why don't I call a strike?'

Like 'em or loathe 'em, ballots are here to stay. Fortunately, the unions have adapted to them better than the employers or the courts.

# From hurdles to the high jump

Recognition of a trade union is not like bumping into someone in the street and saying 'Hi, I recognise you, you're a trade union'. Or 'Give me a clue – I know I recognise you from somewhere – did we meet at the Joneses the summer before last?' Union recognition is more formal than that.

First they have to be recognised by someone called the certification officer. The reasoning goes that if there wasn't this formal hoop-jumping, any group of oddballs or troublemakers could get together, decide they want to be a union, march into an employer's office and make unreasonable demands. By formalising the process, it means that the oddballs and troublemakers who walk into an employer's office and make unreasonable demands are doing it officially.

There is some sense to the process. Unions and their members enjoy certain legal advantages – like not being fired for simply asking for more money – so formal recognition does have its pluses.

It goes without saying that the benefits of recognition have been eaten away by a series of anti-union laws, as the majority of politicians, particularly Tories, believe that even the most placid, reasonable trade unionist is a troublemaker and every demand is unreasonable, bordering on anarchy.

Getting past the certification officer is the easy part. The problems begin when a union asks to be recognised by an employer it wants to deal with. Just because a union has been around for decades, has thousands of members and represents people in a particular workplace doesn't mean the bosses are going to lay out the welcome mat and put on the kettle. Some may be reasonable but others would rather cut off their heads than accept unions in *their* factory or *their* office (funny, isn't it, how the place of work always belongs to the boss class, rather than the people who actually do the work?).

Employers have a variety of reasons why they don't want to recognise the union. How about 'Why do you need the union in here? We've always got on well together, haven't we?' (Said in a whiney voice to people earning a fraction of the rate paid in unionised parts of their industry.) Or

'I'm sure if the union stays out of it we can come to a good arrangement that will really benefit you'. (Translation: I'll put up your wages now and as soon as the threat of the union has vanished, I'll bring them down again.) Or there is the more rational, honest approach: 'You can tell the union to piss off and you can piss off with them if you don't like it.'

In the old days, the only recourse to be had against an unmovable boss like that was to take industrial action (see the Grunwick dispute, for example, below). Now workers can take part in a ballot where they are simply asked if they wish to be represented by the union. This is a bloody stupid question. Why on earth would they have joined it if they didn't want it to represent them? Did they think it was an offshoot of the National Trust?

It would be nice to be able to say this is a simple procedure: just adding up who says 'Yes' and who says 'No' and coming to an obvious conclusion. But the law on union recognition covers fifty-nine pages of the Employment Act 1999 and was clearly written by lawyers, for lawyers, with fees in mind.

There are all sorts of complications, like who can vote, who can't, what about other unions in the same workplace and possibly even what colour hat the returning officer must wear (that might be true – we wouldn't know because the only people who have got down to the end of the fifty-ninth page are lawyers and we can't afford their fees to find out).

It goes without saying that the bosses will pull every possible trick to get a 'No' vote. Like insisting managers are shop-floor workers so they can take part and delve into the black arts of Divide and Rule.

It takes the most persistent trade unionists to keep on fighting for recognition. But those that do can be satisfied with the race run and the battle won. Until another ballot is called in three years' time to see if the members still want their union to be recognised.

Anyone interested in pursuing this course of action might like to consider alternative ways to spend their time – like pushing eggs uphill with their nose.

# Snapshot of a dispute

Just as the match girls were unlikely industrial warriors in the late nineteenth century, so were the sari-clad women of Grunwick in the long hot summer of 1976. The dispute lasted for almost two years and had a huge influence on Mrs Thatcher as she sat in her bunker preparing for power.

This is how it came about. In the days before digital cameras, when people used to get their films developed, many took the cheap option and sent them to a mail-order processor. Grunwick was one of those. Based in Willes-den, north London, it was owned by an Anglo-Indian, George Ward, who paid his staff as little as he could get away with and provided the barest minimum of facilities within the law.

One afternoon four young men went on a go-slow which led to one being sacked and the other three walking out in sympathy. Four workers gone meant others would have to work overtime. Jaybeen Desai refused and, along with her son Sunil, handed in her notice on the spot. The next Monday Mrs Desai, Sunil and the four other work-ers turned up outside their former place of employment armed with placards, calling on the other workers to join them on strike and sign their petition demanding trade union recognition. At that point, they weren't actually members of a union and it wasn't clear which union they wanted recognition for but after an emergency bike ride to the local Citizens Advice Bureau, the Grunwick Eleven (seven other workers had joined them) became members of the Association of Professional, Executive, Clerical and Computer Staff (APEX).

By the end of August, 137 out of a workforce of almost 500 were on strike. They formed their own strike com-mittee and announced that they would not return to work unless and until Grunwick recognised their newly adopted trade union. In response George Ward declared that the strikers should consider themselves dismissed and simply hired more staff.

As the majority of the workforce carried on working, there was little impact on George Ward's operation so the strikers got support from other unions. Kodak workers refused to supply Grunwick but managers just went out and bought the necessary supplies themselves. Mrs Desai persuaded the postal workers' union to refuse to deliver or collect mail from Grunwick, which made the mail-order business somewhat difficult. At which point George Ward went to court and forced the Post Office to honour its legal obligation to deliver mail, regardless of what its employees might think about one of its customers.

The strike was about to collapse in the same shambolic way it had begun when the strike committee called for a mass picket over several days of action. First to turn up were the Socialist Workers and their comrades, who tried to blockade the factory while the police tried to stop them. Two weeks of violence shown every night on the TV news showed the diminutive, sari-clad Mrs Desai apparently taking on 'the bosses' while a bunch of 'leftie hooligans' battled with the police. Grunwick was *the* place to be if you were a trade unionist, a left-wing student or simply fancied being part of something that looked quite exciting and revolutionary in that glorious summer.

The pickets blamed the police, the police blamed the

JO PHILLIPS & DAVID SEYMOUR

pickets. Grunwick hired buses to bring its workers in and protect them from the pickets. The TUC and APEX were not hugely enthusiastic about the image such coverage gave the unions and asked the Grunwick strikers to call off the day of action. They refused. Meanwhile, the postal workers were defying the court order and refusing to handle mail for Grunwick. Then Arthur Scargill decided the National Union of Mineworkers should lend their support. (In case you have forgotten, this was all over a small plant developing holiday snaps.) A crowd of some 20,000 overwhelmed the police, blockaded the plant and stopped Grunwick from bussing in its staff. By mid-morning, everyone had left Willesden to join a protest march, leaving a handful of pickets behind who couldn't stop the plant resuming normal operations.

The strike was failing, and the courts moved to stop other unions supporting the strikers. Mrs Desai was furious with what she saw as the trade union movement's weakness so she organised a hunger strike outside the TUC. APEX finally lost patience and suspended the strikers from the union. The strikers struggled on for a bit but finally admitted defeat after 670 days. Grunwick never recognised the union and none of the strikers was ever reinstated.

It had been a shambolic, chaotic muddle but has gone down in union mythology as a seminal battle. It was, but not in a positive way for the unions. It also showed the

Labour government and the union establishment to be embarrassed by what was portrayed as 'extremism'. And there were mutterings that the union leaderships, being overwhelmingly white and male, exhibited signs of sexism and racism. Being faced with Asian women on strike, the unions were made to realise they were out of kilter with Britain's changing workforce.

# Just our Bill

When Bill Morris was at school in Jamaica, his teacher asked him what he would like to do. He replied that he would like to play cricket professionally. The teacher laughed and asked how he could possibly think the impoverished son of a single-parent family might achieve that.

What would that teacher have said if Bill's reply had been 'I would like to become the first black leader of one of the greatest British trade unions and first black chairman of the TUC, as well as a director of the Bank of England. I would like to be knighted, too, and go on to be a member of the House of Lords'?

Laughable, eh? Yet Lord Morris of Handsworth has not only surmounted those pinnacles but has been a member of so many leading organisations and chaired so many bodies and inquiries that there isn't room to print them all.

He has been pretty much a one-off, though. The union movement is still almost exclusively dominated at the highest levels by white males.

Bill Morris did it without recourse to positive discrimination – he got where he was through his own personality and hard work (even fighting off a plot by people around Tony Blair to prevent his being re-elected as general secretary of the T&G). Perhaps other potential black leaders need a bit of help to get anywhere near where he did.

# Boring stuff

Sorry about this, but no book about the unions is complete without a guide to the labyrinthine nature of how they work. It doesn't have to be like that but the sort of people who run them, in common with the sort of people who run most organisations, have a pathological need for rules and rule books, procedure, bureaucracy and meetings.

The good news is that, as an ordinary union member, you aren't compelled to immerse yourself up to the eyeballs in it all, let alone over the top of your head so you feel as if you are drowning in points of order, rule 87(b), subsection iii, clauses 3–7 or the intense politics involved in deciding who will be chosen as the assistant branch minutes secretary at the next AGM.

A shocked union member discovers that rule 18, sub-section 6(ii) bans people with beards from branch meetings.

On the other hand, it will help if you know vaguely what is going on so you can at least have a bit of a grasp of what is happening. So here is *The Vague Guide to Trade Unions*.

★ Unions have members.

★ Members will be in a workplace branch if where they work has enough people in the union. The officials who run this part of the union are called shop stewards, though there will be other office holders in bigger workplace organisations. There will be a committee. Where there's a union, there's a committee.

★ All the members in a particular area or region will be

in, unsurprisingly, a regional or area section of the union. There will be a chairman of the branch, plus a secretary, treasurer and so on. And a committee.

★ The national union. This is the Big One. There will be a general secretary, president, treasurer and various other officers. And a really serious committee. It is usually called the National Executive, but it's only a committee really. The officials will be full time and receiving salaries from the union. Members of the Executive will be in the major unions, too.

The theory is that, on the whole, issues arise at workplace level and can be dealt with there if they aren't too problematic. If they are, they will be referred up to the branch. And then possibly to head office so a big hitter can come in, thump the desk and sort out the management (or the members).

There is a misconception that the members on the shop floor are almost all mild, sensible folk and that it is the head office thugs who are the intransigent troublemakers. This is not necessarily so. Quite often the officials lower down the pecking order are the ones who are really militant and they feel that the national officers are too quick to want to compromise.

Being vague about how unions operate is actually a necessity, as no two are exactly the same. A certain amount will depend on who the shop stewards and branch officers are – some will insist on heavy-duty organisation while others will be content with a more laid-back way of doing things.

The majority of people aren't interested in the minutiae of running bodies like unions – the same is true of politics. But remember this: if it weren't for those who do the donkey work, however much of a perverse kick they get from it, these organisations wouldn't exist and wouldn't be there when you need them.

## You *can* always get what you want

On a simple scale, every family is regularly involved in negotiations.

TEENAGE DAUGHTER: Can I go out tonight?

FATHER: No.

TD: Oh please. I promise to be home by eleven.

F: You are supposed to be revising for your GCSEs.

TD: I'll get most of it done before I go out and I can finish the rest in the morning.

F: What time are you supposed to be going out? (*This is the first sign of weakness. A crucial moment in any negotiation, as every union official and teenage daughter knows.*)

TD: It's supposed to be seven but I could make it 7.30. . .

F: Hmmm.

TD: . . . or 7.45.

F: Make it eight.

TD: It's a deal! Thanks, Dad.

So that is all there is to negotiation. Especially if the person you are negotiating with can be twisted round your little finger and given a peck on the cheek every time you win. (Important note to putative union negotiators: do NOT, repeat NOT, attempt to kiss any member of the management at the conclusion of negotiations. Or, for that matter, during them.)

Union negotiations can be big official talks, perhaps involving senior officers of the national union, or local discussions in which shop stewards or branch officials handle things.

Local talks can be an almost continuous process in large companies. The firm will have people in the human resources department whose main function is dealing with the unions, while the union(s) will have officers who spend much, sometimes all, of their working life dealing with management. In fact, they are as essential to the smooth running of the company as the people called management.

The idea that these officials are petty dictators, as portrayed so brilliantly by Peter Sellers in the film *I'm*

*All Right Jack,* is very old fashioned. Often it is some of the brightest and most dynamic employees who perform union duties and sensible management understand that. In fact, many union officials go on to take management jobs. This is not selling out, as silly colleagues may say, but a perfectly obvious progression (however, see 'Kiss my arse' on pages 158–61).

When plant-level talks deal with major issues, such as pay, they aren't much different from the times when the big boys come in (not many girls, even though most women are far better at getting what they want). The techniques are similar, though obviously the national officials have an experience gained from years of bargaining as well as almost continual involvement in negotiations.

Some of the devices used by legendary negotiators have passed into folk lore. They are the acceptable equivalent of the Gestapo shining a bright light in your face and sneering: 'Now – talk!'

They include:

★ Move the chairs put out for your team in a purposeful way. The implication of this is that the management has been trying to pull a fast one, you are onto it and they aren't going to get away with it.

★ If it is a sunny day, insist that the management negotiators face the window, so the sun is in their eyes.

★ Try to get your chairs higher than theirs. There is an important psychological advantage in appearing bigger than your opponent.

★ Don't let them finish making their case. When they go into why they shouldn't agree to your demands, stop them halfway through and dismissively brush aside their argument, as if it isn't worth listening to.

★ Start the meeting by going over your case in excruciating detail in a soliloquy that goes on and on and on. The sheer boredom of this will grind them down. *Or*

★ Do the opposite, particularly if at previous meetings you have opened by boring for Britain. This time, simply say: 'You know our case, what's your answer?' This will completely throw them. They were expecting to have at least a couple of hours to work out what they were going to say.

★ Be reasonable. This is especially effective if previous negotiations have involved a lot of haranguing of management. If this time you suddenly are all sweetness and mild reason, they may actually give you what they have refused before because they are so incredibly grateful not to have to suffer your abuse any more. If this gratitude extends to things like asking if you would like to be their grandchild's godfather, say 'No'.

★ Do a Mutt and Jeff, sometimes known as Good Cop–

Bad Cop. One of you is beastly, shouts and is totally unreasonable. Then, when management look like bursting into tears, the other one of you comes in all sweet kindness. Rarely fails, even if the bosses know jolly well what you are up to.

★ Walk out unexpectedly. This may be done in an apparent fit of pique or it could just be getting up, saying 'We're going to have to put this to our members' and going.

★ Always, but always, have the last word.

Negotiating is one of the great skills in life, as you may by now have gathered. Anyone can go in to see management and get walked all over, but it takes real ability, ruthlessness and experience to be a successful negotiator.

Generations of union members have had good reason to thank their representatives for what they have achieved, though they rarely completely appreciate just how difficult their job has been.

The satisfaction for the ace negotiator is not just winning but in defeating the bosses and their highly paid, supposedly competent team. There is a special pleasure in dealing with a new, usually young, inexperienced manager who believes he knows everything and will score an easy triumph over those union people, who he considers to be simpletons. Thrashing this section of the boss class is too easy – genuinely like taking candy from a baby. They are so dumb they think they have won – until they go back to the big bosses and report on what has been 'achieved' and get screamed at and abused for being so unbelievably naïve.

# From closed to closed down

After fighting for decades to gain recognition from employers, unions managed to swing the balance of power in the other direction.

They created the closed shop, which meant that everyone who worked in a particular firm had to be a member of the union. In some cases that meant not just becoming a member once they got the job, but having to be one to get in. So if you weren't in the union, you couldn't get the job.

That made it difficult – if not impossible – for people who weren't in a union to get certain work. It was, however, enormously good for the unions and their members, as it meant union membership was practically a guarantee of work and the unions would have large memberships. In the mafia, it was called a protection racket.

The bosses didn't like it and looked for someone to make the unions an offer they couldn't refuse. Apart from anything else, the closed shop made them feel powerless.

They believed it was their God-given right to hire and fire at will, and the closed shop prevented them from doing that. Though the unions denied that, using the Henry Ford defence. He said 'You can have any colour as long as it's black'; the unions said 'You can have any worker as long as he's one of ours'.

The Elliot Ness the bosses had been looking for turned up in the unlikely figure of – all together now – Margaret Thatcher. The closed shop was one of her first targets. Since then it has been illegal to refuse employment to someone because they aren't in a union or won't join one.

This law has been central to undermining unions, particularly in the private sector. It has allowed bosses once again to play their favourite game of 'Divide and Rule.' (It's astonishing that Waddington's have never made a board game called that. It might rival Monopoly.) Employers can turn down the union's claim for a pay rise but give it just the same to those workers who aren't in the union. They may even avoid making non-union employees redundant when jobs have to go, as long as they don't make it too obvious (see 'Victims of hate' on pages 144–6).

The only thing to be grateful for is that Thatcher didn't call the banning of the closed shop the Right to Work Act, as the Americans did. If ever there were a wrongly named law, this is it. It sounds as if it gives everyone the right to work but is simply a nasty piece of anti-union legislation.

The closed shop is gone but its demise carries a lesson. Whenever the workers and unions find an effective tactic, the politicians will ban it. On behalf of their pals, the bosses.

# The closed shop: a musical interlude

Among the last closed shops were the Musicians' Union and Equity, which represents actors, darling.

Musicians' pay rates are set by the union and vary according to whether you're an accompanist, gigging at a holiday centre, an organist in London, playing in a pub, performing on a ship or on tour with an opera and ballet company. Equity has different rates for national, local rep, BBC and ITV and it doesn't matter if you're a Hollywood superstar, when you tread the boards in London's West End you'll be on the Equity rate for the job.

Actors, musicians, broadcasting technicians and camera crews have succeeded in cutting *Coronation Street* to a skeleton staff, scuppering storylines in *Emmerdale* and cancelling TV coverage of the Miss World contest.

In 1979, as if all the other strikes weren't bad enough, TV was pretty much closed down for weeks due to industrial action by technicians.

In 1961, when there wasn't much on TV anyway, Equity whacked in a demand for thirty-six guineas – equal to a

260 per cent pay rise – while for an actor who had more than ten lines they wanted forty-four guineas, or a 340 per cent rise. ITV wouldn't budge, so the union instructed its members not to sign new contracts and consequently several characters in *Coronation Street* were lost forever while the soap limped on for five months with just fourteen characters. Programmes like *The Avengers* and *Emergency Ward 10* – which was a bit like *Casualty* without the sex and violence – vanished from the screens during the strike and the schedules were filled with American imports. What excuse have the schedulers for putting out the same diet of shows today?

Cameramen walked out during *A Song for Europe* (frankly, who could blame them?) leaving TV coverage in sound only. Of course, when Black Lace won, the crews realised it would have been better to kill the sound and leave the pictures on.

There's something slightly odd about the idea of an orchestra's principal violinist also being a militant shop steward but just because a talented musician, actor or artist is lucky enough to follow their vocation shouldn't mean it's OK to exploit them.

Record companies, agents and promoters have ripped off and exploited artists for years but the internet has allowed many budding – and indeed, established – musicians to do their own sales and marketing direct to fans.

The days of performing for the fun of it and a couple of pints at the end have gone but the Musicians' Union has been instrumental (sorry) in campaigning to protect and support live music in pubs, clubs and theatres.

# Buy one collective bargain, get one free

The world stands on its head in its attitude towards management and unions negotiating over a deal. Usually it is the bosses who want to be free and unfettered by rules, regulations and, particularly, government interference, while unions and the Labour movement are generally addicted to the state sticking its finger in every possible pie.

But when it comes to negotiations, it is the unions whose battle cry is for 'free collective bargaining', meaning free from government meddling, while companies are keen for the talks to be controlled.

The whole expression is rather outdated and peculiar when you consider it. Calling talks to settle pay and conditions 'bargaining' makes it sound as if it is haggling over the price of a carpet in a Turkish bazaar. It may have been like that long, long ago, but it certainly hasn't been for some time.

'Collective' obviously applies to the involvement of the union. As in 'a collective of workers', but when was the last time you heard them referred to like that? Probably in the middle of the nineteenth century, if your memory stretches back that far.

Then there is 'free'. It must have first been used because union negotiators wanted to feel that everything was up for grabs when they went in to open talks with management. At various times in the twentieth century, governments laid down a pay limit. Unions could negotiate as much as they liked, but their members wouldn't get more than X per cent. It hardly seemed worth bothering going through all the argy-bargy. Employers were unlikely to offer less than the laid-down figure and employees weren't going to get more. There might have been bargaining round the edges, on things like allowances, for example, but the negotiations were certainly not free.

During such times, both sides managed to create clever ways to get around the restrictions laid down by the government. In some companies, everyone (almost) would be promoted. The pay limit could be breached if someone was appointed to a more senior role, so there would be a rash of people being given fancy titles (such as Head of Paper Clips or Director of Telephones or Senior Manager, Stairwells) so they could have their salaries raised. And there was nothing the government and its wage spies could do about it. There would also be the introduction of crucial new allowances, so while a pay rise was limited to, say, 5 per cent, management would suddenly realise, with a bit of prodding from union negotiators, that it was essential for everyone to have a special Envelope Allowance, so they could send company letters from home should an emergency arise.

One of the positive things about Mrs Thatcher's reign of terror was that she was opposed to government interference in just about anything, so free collective bargaining was given its head.

For those interested in such arcane matters, there is a theory that collective bargaining is a human right deduced from the Universal Declaration of Human Rights. However, this appears to be pushing it. Free collective bargaining is simply a weapon in the union armoury and the many restrictions placed on them in other areas means it will never again be as free as it used to be.

# Money, money, money (it's a rich man's world)

Mainly thanks to unions, every year workers who have been the victims of accidents or unfair treatment receive around £330 million in compensation. That's quite a lot of money, though the amount individuals receive is rarely as life-changing as the event which led to the compensation.

Anyone who is able to pick up a reasonable sum and walk into another comparable job after a restorative holiday in the sun is going to be very fortunate. Usually what they get has to last for a long time and in most cases they will end up being worse off once the money runs low.

So it is sickening to see pay-outs to workers who have gone through some form of commercial hell being treated in the papers as if the money is a bonanza akin to winning the Lottery.

As ever, it isn't the ordinary people who are the big beneficiaries from pay-outs and compensation, but the guys at the top. It is, as Abba sang with such insight, a rich man's world.

While the shop-floor worker will be awarded a few thousand for loss of earnings after a bad accident or remorseless victimisation from a beastly boss, chairmen, chief executives and other senior executives can completely foul up what they are supposed to be doing, lose the company a fortune, and still walk away with millions. Each. Not shared out among all the hopeless directors.

The thinking behind the usually low level of compensation for workers is that the amount they get shouldn't be a windfall, just enough to make up for the money they have lost through whatever it is has happened to them.

With bosses, the excuse for them receiving so much is that they, too, are merely getting what they would have been entitled to under their contracts. But this takes no account of (a) their contracts being for obscene amounts of money and (b) the fact that as they have been sacked because they failed to do what they were being paid all that money for, they shouldn't really be entitled to anything.

If ordinary workers got compensation at the same level as bosses, and the £330 million a year rose to £33 billion, there wouldn't be many examples of people being forced to sue for victimisation, unfair dismissal and the rest.

# I fought the law and the law won

If you are thinking of taking a long, complicated and expensive course in trade union law, don't bother. We can save you a lot of time and money.

Here is all you need to know about the law and unions: when a disagreement comes to court, the union loses. That's it. There is a slight amendment to that simple legal fact. Occasionally a union member might win. But that is only when he, or she, is taking action against a union. If they are fighting a company or their employers, they will lose.

Despite that basic and consistently followed rule, great books are written about trade union law and judges, especially the highest (and most experienced) in the land, pontificate for days about what they call 'the law'. What they are actually doing is thinking of a way for the union to lose, even when it is patently obvious to any right-minded person (a favourite phrase of judges) that the union should walk away with the case and the bosses haven't got a legal leg to stand on.

The greatest absurdity of modern times came when BA took the union Unite to court claiming that a strike ballot was unlawful. This claim was based on the failure of the union to tell members that eleven ballot papers had been spoilt – that is eleven out of 11,691. And the members voted to strike by 78.77 per cent.

You might think that is a pretty clear mandate (though an earlier court hearing insisted it wasn't for some other arcane reason) but the fact that less than 0.1 per cent of members didn't know how to write an X and that information wasn't passed on to the other 11,680 (although it was posted on the website) was enough for a judge to say the ballot was void.

That was such a gob-smackingly absurd decision that the Court of Appeal was shamed into overturning it, a legal first. But have no fear, next time they will be back to supporting some other legal insanity to prevent workers striking or doing anything else which might not be in the bosses' very best interests.

After decades, even centuries, of struggle, a right to strike was won and the courts were somewhat sidelined when it came to industrial disputes. This changed with the Margaret Thatcher–Norman Tebbit union laws, which gave the biggest pay rises ever to a select group of working people – employment lawyers.

If ever you can't sleep, far better than counting sheep is reading the Trade Union and Labour Relations (Consolidation) Act 1992, which pulls together all the Thatcher laws and runs to 303 sections as well as three schedules.

Should you manage to get to Section Three and still be awake, you are seriously an insomniac. (Try this in Section Two: 'The Certification Officer shall keep a list of trade unions containing the names of (a) the organisations whose names were, immediately before the commencement of this Act, duly entered in the list of trade unions kept by him under section 8 of the [1974 c. 52] Trade Union and Labour Relations Act 1974. . .' and so on for another five sub-clauses.)

The Act covers every conceivable thing a union might do and a lot they probably wouldn't dream of doing. Its aim is to make life so difficult for workers who want to be in a union and particularly when they want to take industrial action that they become so discouraged they decide they might as well go off to the pub instead or stay in watching *Jeremy Kyle*, where the dysfunctional participants, incredibly, appear to have more connection with real life.

# You're not wanted any more

The perfect relationship between employer and worker, from the boss's point of view, is that he can hire when he wants and then fire his employee, no matter how long he has worked for him, at the company's convenience.

It was like that for a long time, with loyal and committed workers suddenly being thrown out on the streets, with nothing more than their pay until the end of the week.

The introduction of redundancy laws by the Labour government in the 1960s not only forced employers to pay compensation but laid down that they must consider alternatives before making people redundant.

This is something of a sham, it must be said. If a company has decided it is going to cut its staff by 10 per cent, it can go through all sorts of pretend consultations but is unlikely to change its mind.

However, it does at least have to talk to the unions which represent the employees it plans to fire. It may be possible for them to bring down the number of workers who have to go, to increase the redundancy pay-outs – there is a statutory figure laid down but firms can have their arm twisted to add a bit more – and, most importantly, they can negotiate over who is to go.

Whenever there is a proposed redundancy, there will

always be some employees who volunteer to go. Maybe they have had enough of that firm, maybe they want to retire, maybe they want to change careers and switch from answering phones in a call centre to becoming a portrait painter. If redundancy can be restricted to volunteers, no one is forced out and those who do go are doubly happy because they have got out with cash in their pockets.

Compulsory redundancy is nasty and unions fight tooth and nail to prevent it. Even with reasonably generous pay-outs (and they aren't that common) it is a bitter blow to be forced out of your job, especially when the prospect of getting another one is remote. If you are one of a thousand people thrown out of a factory, you are one of a thousand people looking for work. It's going to be tough finding a new job and while redundancy pay makes life easier for a while and means you don't immediately have to worry about money, it isn't going to last forever, unless you are close to retirement.

But if it hadn't been for the unions and the Labour Party, there still wouldn't be redundancy pay.

# The hour has come

A row has been going on about the European Union's insistence on a shorter working week. Bosses have objected. Many politicians have protested. Even some workers have rung up phone-ins to rant about 'European meddling' which will prevent them driving their lorries for 100-plus hours a week or doing some other job that could be lethal if carried out by an exhausted employee.

There is nothing new about workers wanting shorter hours. It is not an invention of 21st-century meddlers based in Brussels. In fact, the first demand of the TUC was for a fixed eight-hour day. And that was in the 1860s. Would those early trade unionists have believed that a century and a half later, the struggle would still be going on?

Probably because the disputes that usually hit the headlines involve pay, the role that unions have played in getting working conditions improved are easily forgotten. Often these are negotiated with individual employers but the TUC has been instrumental in pushing governments to give workers' rights the rule of law.

Long before the rise of capitalism and the Industrial Revolution, workers were exploited. Long hours, few days off and rare (if any) holidays. The working lifestyle enjoyed by millions today is almost exclusively due to the work of the unions.

Don't ever think the bosses gave these rights voluntarily. They fought with all their might to prevent them. If there were no unions and working conditions were entirely at the discretion of employers, they'd still be sending little boys up chimneys. That is, after all, for the boys' own good – the pennies they can earn avoid their families starving.

# Victims of hate

Just as it is difficult for people who haven't suffered an abusive personal relationship to fully grasp how terrible that can be, so it is with a really nasty boss. You hear it excused as 'just a bit of banter' or 'the way things are at work'. No it isn't.

To have to go into work every day knowing you are going to suffer taunts, abuse and sheer nastiness is horrible. You need the job, you need the money, why should you be driven out? But that may seem like the only way to end the misery. Sometimes it is due to a manager – or maybe just a work colleague, though 'colleague' is not the way to describe someone who behaves like that – not liking you or being jealous or feeling threatened by your ability.

It is when the bullying is carried out for a purpose by the employer that it becomes victimisation. It may be that a worker is a union official or simply active in the union. Or that he has raised a complaint about a line manager or something he has been asked to do. It doesn't have to be blatant abuse. It could be refusing to promote an employee because he has started a grievance procedure or given evidence for a colleague at a tribunal.

Victimisation isn't always obvious abuse. It may be that someone is refused time off deliberately to make working life impossible for them to square with their family commitments or be refused promotion or training that will help them get promoted. They may be ignored – not given any work – continually criticised or sniped at. They may be the constant butt of snide comments and 'jokes' made to other workers, who feel they have to laugh or they will become victims themselves.

What should be the basic right of every worker to get on with the job without harassment and with as much flexibility and encouragement as possible for them and the company becomes an attempt to make their lives such a misery that they are driven out of the job.

There are few areas in which unions and employment law have moved further to protect workers than that of victimisation. A successful appeal to an employment tribunal can result in substantial damages. What remains extraordinary is that so many of these cases that you read about in the paper end with the employee getting a payoff but with their working life wrecked, while the bullying manager stays in his (or her) job.

In theory, the victimised employee should be offered his job back. It rarely happens. What the law ought to say is that the bully should be sacked. If they have done it to one subordinate, the chances are they will do it to another.

And the next one – or ones – may not be prepared to get involved in a long battle, so just walk away, their working life in tatters.

While it is clearly good that workers can be compensated for being victimised, the law still maintains the master/servant relationship by refusing to punish the person who did it. Though when it comes to victimisation for union work, it is pretty obvious it is being done with the management's connivance, perhaps even at its instruction. It is sickening to think they can still get away with it by paying the victim a bit of blood money.

# Elf and fairy stories

Health and safety has become a joke thanks to the mocking of right-wing commentators and the over-zealousness of petty bureaucrats christened 'Elf 'n' Safety'.

Of course some of the edicts they lay down are absurd and they do no one any favours by pushing things to an extreme. But there is nothing to laugh about in health and safety at work. Workers still die when they are simply doing their job and half a million still suffer some form of work-related injury or illness every year.

It would be good to present you with statistics comparing today's figures for accidents at work with those of, say, a century ago. This is not possible. No statistics were collected until comparatively recently because accidents and work went together like hand and glove or, more accurately, executioner and axe. If you went to work, there was a reasonable chance you would end up maimed or dead. This didn't, of course, apply to bosses.

Today, despite the Health and Safety at Work Act and the Health and Safety Executive and health and safety officers in all major workplaces, there are still far too many people hurt or killed when they are just trying to earn a living.

Building work remains dangerous and so does agriculture. The average number of people killed is still around 200 a year. But there are at any one time about 1.2 million workers suffering from illnesses caused or made worse by their work.

Around thirty million days are lost to British industry every year due to work-related ill-health and 4.7 million to workplace injury alone. That is an awful lot of nonproductive days.

Unions have been crucial in raising the importance to working people of providing a safe environment and without their pressure the likelihood is that the deaths and injuries would be many times higher. Remember that next time you hear someone mocking 'Elf 'n' Safety'.

A silver lining in dark days: there is one bit of good

news about the recession. When the economy slides downwards, research shows that there are not just fewer accidents at work but a lower percentage of accidents among those still working. So be cheered by the thought that, if you manage to keep your job, you are less likely to be hurt at work. A double win!

# Inhuman resources

The management people that unions usually deal with work in a department called Human Resources. It used to be called Personnel but sometime around the 1970s some bright spark – almost certainly an American 'management guru' – decided a more touchy-feely name would be better.

Better for what? Did they think that union representatives or individual workers faced with some hatchet-faced manager who was telling them they were about to lose their job or have their hours increased would say: 'I may not like what they are telling me but they must be OK guys because they work in Human Resources'? Don't think so.

The name is actually quite revealing. It doesn't mean to imply that the people in the department are human. That would be going too far. These are individuals who learn about being human from books. Books like 'How to be human' and 'Learn how to be human in ten days' or 'Teach yourself human'.

No, the expression *human resources* applies to what they do. They deal with company resources. As there are managers who take care of the computers or machinery or the canteen, HR are responsible for the people-machines. What is most repulsive about their job title is that human resources remove the humanity from dealing with the workforce.

They always refer to themselves as HR because it is only one letter short of HRH – Her Royal Highness. They think this is appropriate because human resources are the near-royalty of industry (royalty being the chief executive and other directors).

Here is a word of advice for new union reps contemplating dealing with HR on a regular basis: consider other less masochistic ways of spending your time. Like banging your head repeatedly against a brick wall. Or nailing your fingers to a table. Or pulling your teeth out with pliers.

## Labour pains

As the union movement is to a great extent discounted nowadays as an aged crone in a modern world or perhaps a dysfunctional old uncle, babbling away to himself in a corner, it is worth remembering that once it was the proud parent of a bonny young political party.

Without the unions there would be no Labour Party and even its detractors must admit that the history of this country over the past century would have been very different if it had never existed.

This is how the conception came about. In the later years of the nineteenth century, as the unions became better organised, they realised that although they had succeeded in getting the vote for the working man, there was no party suitable for him to vote for (working women didn't get the vote until a lot later, as everyone who has assiduously read our earlier book, *Why Vote?*, will know).

They couldn't vote for the Tories. That was the party of the bosses. And the Liberals may have been liberal but were very much a party of the middle classes.

So the TUC set about putting that right. In 1900, as a new century dawned bringing with it enormous hope of peace and prosperity (to be followed shortly by World War One and the Great Depression), the unions established a Labour Representation Committee.

That wasn't entirely because they didn't feel confident about going the whole hog and actually establishing a new political party nor because they were – and remain – besotted with committees (see 'Boring stuff' on pages

122–5). No, the union leaders wanted to keep some kind of control over what was happening. Some hope!

From its inception, the LRC presented the same sort of shambolic lack of organisation that was to almost destroy the Labour Party eighty years later. It didn't have a leader, for a start, and at the election in October 1900 spent a mere £33, which was 0.0003 per cent of the amount Labour blew on the election a century later.

In 1910, twenty-nine Labour MPs were elected and fourteen years later the party formed a government for the first time. Much has changed since then but the unions were essential to the running of the party for most of that time and remain crucial to its funding.

In government and out, the big union leaders continued to dominate Labour. Not only did they have guaranteed seats on the party's National Executive, they were the only ones who mattered at the annual seaside conferences. The unions had block votes. This meant that a union with 1.5 million members had 1.5 million votes. A constituency delegate sent by his local Labour party had one thousand votes, due to a peculiar quirk which assumed that all constituencies had a thousand members, even if they only had three. So if the general secretary of that union held up his card in favour of a particular motion, it would need 1,501 constituency parties to outvote him. As there were not much more than a third of that number of local parties, it meant the union barons always won. Unless different unions voted against each other, which happened rather often.

This may sound ludicrous, chaotic and absurd, and it was. It was no way to run a party, particularly when that party was supposed to be running the country, which Labour was occasionally allowed to do. Eventually this system was replaced by a sort of one member–one vote procedure, though it's not quite as simple as that. Nothing in the Labour Party is simple.

Although down the years Labour governments have introduced important laws for the benefit of working people, there have been many occasions when union members must wonder whether it really is worth supporting a party which can seem to be more interested in helping very rich bankers than working people struggling to survive.

As for the money the unions continue to lavish on Labour (with a few exceptions), that comes from the members, who make a small weekly payment into what is called the Political Fund. One of the bright ideas Mrs Thatcher had when she was Prime Minister was to make union members vote on whether they wanted to carry on paying this levy, even though it is only a small amount. The bar was set high for getting a 'Yes' vote, her reasoning being that union members would either vote 'No', because they'd rather spend those few pence a week betting on whippet racing or some such, or they'd be so bored they wouldn't vote, which would count as a 'No'. Clever, eh?

However, the TUC really got its act together and ran a brilliant campaign which culminated in an overwhelming 'Yes' vote. So union members were able to continue paying into the political fund and the unions could carry on giving the money to Labour, who in turn threw it in its millions at posh advertising agencies, spin doctors and glib marketing manipulators.

That's democracy, folks.


# Hard-pressed

No one, but no one, hates the unions more than the press. Their loathing is pathological. To read the papers, you would think that every union leader was on a par with Hitler and Stalin combined, and their members brain-dead militants who need little urging to join the revolution that will bring the country to its knees unless the white knight of the press rides in on its charger to save the world.

The reason the papers behave like this isn't just because they are owned, run and edited by extremely right-wing people (though that helps) but because for a long time they were made mugs of by the print unions.

Napoleons of the printed word such as Beaverbrook,

JO PHILLIPS & DAVID SEYMOUR

Northcliffe and Rothermere – all Lords, in case you didn't know or understand how Prime Ministers show their appreciation for rabid support – paraded in public as if they were all-powerful. And it is true that politicians did quake before the harlots of the fourth estate.

But when dealing with the unions in their own organisations, they melted like the ice in a gin and tonic on a scorching day.

Next time you read a hysterical report of a strike or a mouth-foaming column savaging industrial action and wonder what form of mental illness makes people have such delusions, consider how the newspaper industry used to operate until quite recently.

The unions ran everything. They chose who could work, pretty well when they worked and certainly how the operation ran. Most especially, they chose how much money poured into the overall pockets of their members.

In the pre-computer era (note to younger readers: yes, there was a time when computers didn't exist), the words written by journalists had to be set on wonderful old machines in lines of lead. The men (always men) who set the words were on to one of the best fiddles ever devised outside of investment banking. This how the fantastic system worked:

The compositors, as they were called, got paid by the

line. How much they received was set down in an agreement called the London Scale of Prices. Every conceivable piece of work had a going rate. Nothing was left to the imagination – though plenty of imagination was used in devising ways to extort money from the employers. The bigger the type, the more they got. So setting a headline was paid more than a line of type in a story.

But that was just the start of it. They got paid each time they set something, however often they had to set the same thing. Here is an example (and this went on every day, in every national newspaper office, over and over again). Let us say the price for setting a headline was £1 and the headline was TORIES BEAT OFF ATTACK. When it is set, it just fails to fit in the space allocated to it. So it becomes TORIES BEAT OFF ATTA. The sub-editors, seeing that the headline 'busts', change it to TORIES BEAT ATTACK. It fits! And the compositors get paid another pound. Then the night editor sees the headline, doesn't like it and rewrites it as HEATH BEATS ATTACK (Heath being the Tory Prime Minister of the time). Another pound. But the compositor, in his boredom at doing it again, or maybe for pecuniary reasons, sets it as HAETH BEATS ATTACK. The proof readers spot this and send it back to be reset again to get the name of the Prime Minister correct. Another pound. But now the editor sees the headline, he doesn't want to name Heath in a positive way because he hates him (editors are like that), so changes it back to TORIES BEAT ATTACK. Yet another pound! That means the compositors have made £5 just for one headline. No wonder they were the highest paid blue-collar workers in British industry until Rupert Murdoch came along.

The other section of newspaper workers were the printers who, as their name implies, were responsible for printing the papers. They had a different fiddle altogether. They didn't get paid by what they did, they got paid full stop, whether they turned up for work or not. And mainly it was not.

Let's say it needed ten men (yes, all men again) to operate one press. The union had negotiated that it actually required forty-eight. So what did the other thirty-eight do? Mainly, nothing except get paid. Some wouldn't turn up at all, just pick up their shift money the next time they came in. Others would pop in, be told they weren't needed and go straight home – or to the pub. Though they still got paid. Others would do half a shift, although being paid for a full one. So it was possible to pick up hundreds of pounds a week (a lot of moolah in those days) for doing only a very few hours' work.

Then there were the ghost workers. With fake names like Donald Duck, John Wayne or, for those who liked to sail really close to the wind, Lassie or even Lord Beaverbrook. And they always got paid because if an objection was made, the printers would walk out over some petty pretence and a night's production would be lost. In common with other corrupt union practices (the docks, for one – ever seen *On the Waterfront*? It wasn't only in America that sort of thing happened), some of the loot found its way into the pockets of officials. One union branch secretary had his own private plane.

There was a plethora, a veritable gaggle, of print unions. Two on the presses, for example, who were constantly fighting each other and creating still more problems for the management. One union for making the plates needed to reproduce pictures in the paper and another responsible for the wooden blocks they were mounted on. And so on. Industrial relations on Fleet Street were war by other means with the bosses constantly waving an agreement in the air, Chamberlain-like, proclaiming peace in our time. Until the next time, which would likely be the next night.

Yet the print unions never – or very, very rarely – did anything about the right-wing rantings of the newspapers they produced. As long as they got their big money, the papers could say what they liked. And they did. Especially about unions – though obviously never about the print unions, who had them over a barrel.

It is now many years since unions had any influence in the production of newspapers, yet the hysterical attitude towards them continues with unabated fervour. What is most incredible is that many of their readers are actually members of unions. They read this rubbish accusing them of being devils incarnate yet carry on buying their newspapers. How ridiculous is that?

# Kiss my arse

When Bill Deedes, the legendary *Daily Telegraph* reporter, turned ninety, he was interviewed by a journalist on a trade magazine. During the course of the interview, it was pointed out to him that his son was managing editor on the paper and hence technically his boss. 'What's it like working for your son?' he was asked. Bill's dismissive reply was: 'I never talk about management.'

This is the right attitude and one all young, and not-so-young, workers can learn from. As it happens, Bill Deedes had been an editor himself, but he obviously had never let that elevation interfere with his healthy view of 'management'.

Whereas he had risen to the heights and then slipped back down to doing a proper job, it is quite common for union officials to move in the other direction. The fire-brand negotiator who is thumping the table and giving the company team hell one week may be sitting on the other side of the table by the time the next set of negotiations come around.

Is that so surprising? Only to diehards who have a Them and Us attitude to trade unionism. Just as grammar schools and universities are seen as the vehicles which can help a working-class kid rise up the ladder, so involvement in the union may.

The smart young guy (or gal) who makes their way up the union hierarchy and distinguishes themselves with the professional way they act on behalf of their members, or even their grasp of difficult issues during negotiations, is going to catch the eye of good management people (there are some, you know). Cynics say it is rather a matter of having them on your side than against you. But intelligent managers, particularly those who understand an industry and haven't just come out of university without knowing anything except when the next tutorial is, are hard to come by. The experience and knowledge gained working for the union can be put to good use for the sake of the company.

This leap from one side to the other has been immortalised in the song, to be sung to the tune of 'The Red Flag': 'The working class can kiss my arse, I've got the boss's job at last.'

A different transformation awaits some union officials. They move into politics. The young John Prescott was a shop steward in the National Union of Seamen and was denounced by the then Labour Prime Minister, Harold Wilson, as one of 'a small group of politically motivated men' who led a strike in the 1960s. Prescott proved he wasn't politically motivated at all by becoming a Labour MP and then deputy Prime Minister to Tony Blair and is now Lord Prescott of Kingston upon Hull.

Alan Johnson was running the postal workers' union when he was parachuted into a safe Labour seat and went on to be Home Secretary. And still the Home Office's letters didn't arrive on time.

At one stage, it was fairly common for officials in some unions – particularly the National Union of Mineworkers – to be found a safe Labour seat when they had completed the requisite number of years at the union-face. They could be spotted in Westminster any evening gathered together at one of the Commons bars, foaming pint in hand, all wearing dark three-piece suits with the gold watch they had received for fifty years' service poking out of the waistcoat pocket. A good retirement scheme for them, not so wonderful for their constituents. Though at least they knew the problems of the people they represented.

Nowadays a few select union leaders make it to 'the other place' and become members of the House of Lords. Current peers include Lord Morris of Handsworth, formerly Bill Morris, leader of the T&G; Baroness Dean of Thornton-le-Fylde, formerly Brenda Dean, leader of the print union SOGAT; Lord Triesman, of the Association of University Teachers; Baroness Symons of Vernham Dean, who ran the First Division civil servants' union; and the recently ennobled Lord Monks, formerly the general secretary of the TUC.

# Of baggage, banners and brass bands

Because the trade union movement is steeped in history, it carries a lot of baggage. And banners. And brass bands. All of which can still be seen – and heard – at the annual Durham Miners Gala (which still takes place every year, even though there hasn't been a mine open in Durham for almost twenty years), as well as the Tolpuddle celebrations and other traditional events. But, rather like the former mills, docks, factories and mines that have been turned into museums, dry ski slopes and housing developments, there's something about the unions that seems past its sell-by date. And that's not about what they do, it's how they parade their noble history of the class struggle as the honest working poor against the bloated capitalist bosses. There's a sense of nostalgia, a yearning for the good old, bad old days of strikes, picket lines and interminable branch meetings where the battle plans were drawn up to keep people in dirty, dangerous, unskilled and unfulfilling jobs. Community life was indubitably better and more vibrant; allotments, brass bands and pigeon racing prospered. But health was worse and life prospects generally pretty grim, particularly for women, who didn't really figure in the male-dominated world of industrial Britain.

The dreams of socialism were finally shattered not by Maggie Thatcher and the collapse of the miners' strike but by Tony Blair. He made it absolutely, painfully clear that he no longer wanted his shiny, super-cool New Labour party to be associated with the embarrassing old relatives in the trade unions. Even though they'd supported the Labour Party financially and practically and would go on bailing out the party when the dodgy City backers drifted back to the Tories.

While there are still people whose eyes well up at memories of strikes and struggles past and have conversations that sound like the Four Yorkshiremen in Monty Python who vied with each other over who had been brought up in the smallest shoe box, the reality is that most people are too busy paying the bills, juggling work and family and social lives while counting the days to the next weekend.

The banners, brass bands and memories are all very well, but they are now just an excuse for a good day out. They have become part of a Labour movement theme park.

This may sound like nonsense but the TUC, recognising that many of the battles of the past have been won (or never can be) and that unions need to ditch their cloth-cap image, is promoting the notion of 'good work', which not surprisingly came out of Sweden around the same time as Abba.

This is the nine-point plan for 'good work' (are you sitting comfortably?):

★ job security
★ a fair share of production earnings
★ co-determination in the company
★ a work organisation for co-operation
★ professional know-how in all work
★ training – a part of work
★ working hours based on social demands
★ equality in the workplace
★ a working environment without risk to health and safety.

If you think that sounds boring, try saying it in Swedish. But it would help employers, workers, the economy, the country, the health of the nation and, yes, the Happiness Index, if industrial sniping, hand-to-hand combat and warfare were no more.

'Good work' is about personal fulfilment, realising

potential, best practice and reducing levels of absence, sickness and stress. Incredibly, in an era when we are supposed to be healthier than ever before, 170 million days a year are lost through people being too ill to go to work. You can bet your P45 that quite a few of those days are 'sickies', which would suggest not just a lack of commitment but the underlying stress, anxiety and psychological effects of being unhappy at work.

Many employers and big organisations already understand the economic benefits of a happy workforce – fewer days lost to sickness and a greater level of productivity. From fresh fruit and flexible working to on-site gyms and crèches, lots of companies recognise these employee 'perks' as an investment in their staff which will benefit the company in the long run. Though singing the company song at the start of each working day, as some Japanese firms like to do, does seem to be taking it a bit far.

# Soap and chocolate

Although 'Dress-down Fridays' and 'At-desk back massages' are recent innovations, the idea of looking after your employees isn't. The Cadbury family, who made a mint out of chocolate (and a chocolate out of mint – or was that Rowntree?), created an entire village

– Bournville near Birmingham – for their employees at the start of the twentieth century. Alongside hundreds of houses were football, cricket and hockey pitches, bowling greens and a lido for outdoor swimming although the lido was closed down in 1970 after complaints about noise from a newly built estate and stringent new health and safety regulations. The Bournville Trust still exists and residents have power over planning and development although rumours that baseball will replace bowls now the chocolate company's owned by Americans have not been confirmed.

Further north on Merseyside, William Lever, a self-made Victorian businessman and philanthropist whose soap factory was the start of the global giant Unilever, believed his workers should share in the wealth they'd helped to create. Appalled by the squalid slums his employees lived in, Lever, inspired by Samuel Smiles's book *Self-Help*, created Port Sunlight, a village with decent housing at reasonable rents for his workers. He also provided schools, a library, institutes and public buildings which the workers could use to improve themselves. In return, they were to 'prove themselves worthy of all this by following a life of sobriety, thrift and the desire for self-improvement', a philosophy assiduously promoted every Monday in the *Daily Mail* by Melanie Phillips.

Other organisations have continued the Cadbury/Lever

tradition of looking after their employees. Companies that are cited as good places to work include John Lewis, which is a co-operative so all staff share in the profits, and the technology giants Google and Microsoft.

At the London HQ of a leading international finance company, there's a whole floor of different restaurants and a shop that even sells gifts and wrapping paper which means you never have to leave the office, even if you've forgotten your wedding anniversary. Is that philanthropy, though, or the cynical cult of corporate life?

BBC staff get 'bisque' days off in some bizarre deal (no, we don't know what it is either but it has nothing to do with shellfish) and after a certain length of service they can take a sabbatical or career break. Luncheon Vouchers may be a throwback to a time when no self-respecting sandwich bar had heard of Panini (nowadays they all speak Panini like natives) but subsidised staff canteens save employees money. Company cars, loans for season tickets and other travel benefits help. Pensions did until firms treated them to slash and burn to save billions. The office tea trolley has been replaced by vending machines or kettles. In fact London Underground staff threatened to strike a few years ago in protest at kettles replacing urns while the BBC and other offices won't allow staff to use a kettle unless they are properly trained. The BA strike early in 2010 ended up being about the company's threat to end the perk of cheap air travel for those who went on strike.

It's a long way from 'Not a minute on the day, Not a penny off the pay'.

# Can't join, shan't join

The most successful unions in the country are sadly ones which ordinary workers can't join. In fact, they don't call themselves unions at all – oh no, that would be demeaning their professional status. They pose as 'professional bodies', presumably to distance themselves from the amateur bodies which represent the majority of workers.

Here are some of these organisations:

**The British Medical Association**. This represents doctors, obviously, and is as good a closed shop as you could wish for. They defend their status by saying that naturally you can't have people wandering in off the streets and operating on patients or giving advice. Though when you consider how the medical profession operates at times, it can seem as hit-and-miss as that. The BMA has used that as a pretext to dictate hours to suit themselves rather than their patients and to get the biggest pay rise of any group of workers in the past decade, with the exception of City bankers.

**The Law Society**. Represents solicitors, so you can imagine what a jolly band that is. It has had things its own way for so long, while fees soared, that the Government eventually had to cut legal aid payments, leaving many solicitors out on the streets selling the *Big Issue*.

**The Bar Council**. If you think the Law Society is a tight-knit band of brothers, the Bar Council, which represents barristers, makes it look wide open. They have two particular advantages going for them. Many leading politicians are barristers – and 'are' is the right tense, as most carry on appearing at the bar even though they are being paid to be MPs – so are not likely to curb their powers, incomes or excesses in any way which will affect their own livelihoods. And, secondly, barristers go on to become judges, who are so important that few politicians, let alone ordinary citizens, are brave enough to stand up to them. The barristers' closed shop was so tight that they wouldn't even let solicitors appear in court, though this has now been prized open a bit, so those second-class (in barristers' eyes) lawyers can represent their clients in person. Though only in the most trivial cases, naturally. For big cases you still need to hire a barrister and for the biggest ones, you need at least two, one of them a Queen's Counsel on massive daily fees. If only all trade unions could be as effective for their members as the Bar Council has been for its.

**The Association of Chief Police Officers.** This represents the 350 most senior police officers in England, Wales and Northern Ireland. Scottish police chiefs do their own thing. ACPO is a remarkably influential and powerful organisation, not that you hear much negativity about it. You are far more likely to read about some group of real trade unionists fighting a minor action than the police chiefs applying the law in a way which will affect the lives of millions of innocent citizens. Though there has been an outcry in certain sections of the press about ACPO's enthusiasm for speed cameras, presumably because they inconvenience editors.

**The Confederation of British Industry.** This used to be referred to as 'the bosses' union' until the CBI objected. They prefer to be called 'the employers' organisation'. Of course it doesn't have to negotiate pay and conditions on behalf of its members – the big bosses are more than capable of doing that themselves. So what the CBI does is pressure the government over things which will affect the incomes of their members, like higher taxes and what they call 'red tape', which is actually such annoying and unnecessary burdens on business as providing maternity leave for employees and keeping up health and safety standards. Every year the CBI holds a conference which is very brief. This brevity shows how busy and important its members are. There is also clearly a limit to how many motions you can discuss on issues vital to modern commerce, such as the restoration of sending children up chimneys and the reintroduction of Victorian sweatshop conditions to British factories.

**Federation of Small Businesses.** This is a sad organisation. Well, anyone who goes around calling themselves small has clearly got an inferiority complex. But they make up for it by claiming that they are the big employers in the country, meaning that though they may not have many people working for them individually, taken together – all those newsagents, corner shops and tiny manufacturing operations – they provide employment for a helluva lot of people. Their pipsqueak voice usually manages to contain a tone of indignation, as in 'Hey, I'm down here, look where you're treading. . . look out! LOOK OUT! Ouch, oh, ouch, you've squashed me again with that latest bit of legislation which the big boys won't notice but will *bankrupt* us.'

There are also a number of organisations which are more like trade unions than those bosses' bodies but they aren't recognised as such. This is because their members are considered to do such important work that they just can't be given the same rights as ordinary unionists.

**The Police Federation of England and Wales** (Scotland on its own again) was set up in 1919 after police had the temerity to go on strike. Until then, they had belonged to the National Union of Police and Prison Officers (known as NUPPO, as in 'If you don't get off the street sharpish, son, you're gonna get a nuppo from me'). When they went on strike, unfortunately the National Union of Burglars, Bag Snatchers, Pimps and Bank Robbers didn't come out in sympathy, crime soared and scores of little old ladies were mown down by horse-drawn cabs because there was no one to help them cross the road. The Police Federation is a union in all but name though its members are banned from taking industrial action, official or unofficial. Though this doesn't stop some of them continuing their usual unofficial actions, such as stopping and searching young black people, fitting up suspects and failing to book the chief constable for driving at 60mph in a 30mph speed limit. And there are privileges to being a member of the Federation – like getting £9.99 off a ticket to Longleat Safari Park or, better still, 25 per cent off a meal at a Little Chef (though officers probably can't go there when on duty).

Another 'union' which is not affiliated to the TUC is the **English Collective of Prostitutes** (is there *no* activity with which the Scots want to be associated with the rest of the UK?). Rather like the CBI, they are not really worried about negotiating improved pay rates but want to cut through the red tape which interferes with their business. For them, this means trying to change the laws which not only criminalise their activities but can endanger them. So, from a moral point of view, the English Collective of Prostitutes has a stronger argument than the CBI for what it is trying to do.

# Lord, bless this union. Please

How working life has changed, not just since the days of the Tolpuddle Martyrs but over the past couple of decades. Today when people talk of working in a sweatshop, they mean having to labour long hours in an air-conditioned office. Just about everyone in this country works in safer, cleaner and healthier environments, thanks largely to the efforts of trade unions. Though does that make us happier at work than we were a generation ago?

The common ground between working people has changed, too. It's really stretching the imagination to think of the clippety-clop of kitten-heeled airline cabin crew walking smartly alongside fellow unionists at Tolpuddle, having smiled insincerely at them en route and checking to make sure seat belts are securely fastened on the coach down to Dorset.

So where do the unions fit today? What can they offer to the millions of people who work for themselves, for small businesses, for people who will change careers several times during their working lives? Have the unions become like the AA – a useful bit of insurance for emergencies but not something you need to get involved in?

In politics and political movements, change comes because of the people who are actively involved. No activists, no involvement, no change. The establishment will win every time. And if the only people who get actively involved in unions judge their success by the number of strikes they have, then the future looks bleak for the movement.

The unions have fought and won terrific battles for better working conditions that have benefited all of us, regardless of whether we are card-carrying members. They have also managed to alienate massive swathes of the population by ruining their journeys to work and holidays, their power supply and their children's education and refusing to empty the bins. The more we become a comfortable, consumer-driven society, the more disconnect there will be with the unions' traditional ways of doing things. Some recognise that; others refuse to.

Fighting to preserve the past is not an option. Ask the miners. Or find anyone who will give up their computer and go back to a manual typewriter. Or, if you still aren't convinced, look at the growth of outsourcing to cheaper, often better-educated, workers in other countries.

None of that means letting employers do what they want with the people who work for them. There will always be some who would be happy to reintroduce to 21st-century Britain the appalling working conditions, gruelling hours and abominable pay that exist in the worst real sweat-shops of the third world today.

Complacency is a natural human failing. Most of us are content to accept what we have and refuse to believe that we could slip back into the sort of lives people had a short time ago. If you think things can only get better, you are going to be in for a nasty shock. There have been incalculable improvements in working conditions and they came from people taking action together. You always achieve more when it comes to standing up to bullies, cheapskates and nasties if you stand shoulder to shoulder against them.

That is what unions are really about. It's worked before and it can work again. Whether it will is up to the people who lead them and the people who join them. And Lord knows, we might need the strength of the unions sooner than we think.

# ANSWERS TO THE POP QUIZ (p. 78)

| | |
|---|---|
| **Manic Street Preachers** | 1985 |
| **Pulp** | Last Day of the Miners' Strike |
| **Ewan MacColl** | Daddy, What Did You Do in the Strike? |
| **Sting** | We Work the Black Seam |
| **Billy Bragg** | Which Side Are You On? |
| **U2** | Red Hill Mining Town |
| **Chumbawamba** | Fitzwilliam |
| **Dire Straits** | Iron Hand |
| **Paul Weller** | Stone's Throw Away |